Praise for *Network Like A Fox*

"I have watched Nancy Fox network for years. Applying her business networking approach has had a favorable impact on how I build my business connections and relationships.

I'm pleased to say that Nancy now has shared all her strategies for networking smarter and more successfully in one must-read book, *Network Like A Fox*."

—WENDY BROWN
SENIOR FINANCIAL ADVISOR, VICE PRESIDENT MERRILL LYNCH

"Nothing is more important in business than powerful relationships. In *Network Like A Fox*, Nancy Fox shows you how to transform humdrum, hit or miss marketing into a fresh, surefire method for building the right relationships with just the right people. Read this book and learn how to network smarter — like a fox!"

—BARBARA CORCORAN, REAL ESTATE INVESTOR, ENTREPRENEUR, FEATURED SHARK ON ABC'S HIT REALITY SHOW, *SHARK TANK*

"Networking is not optional in the new normal of this job economy — it's essential. Candidates must be seen and heard to make a lasting impression and seasoned careerists must continue to cultivate relationships to stay relevant and valuable. Nancy Fox unpacks the art and science of networking with practical action steps that every professional should implement to secure a seat at the table. Her book is a must read from the entry level ranks to the C-Suite."

—CAROLINE DOWD-HIGGINS
DIRECTOR OF CAREER & PROFESSIONAL DEVELOPMENT
AND ADJUNCT FACULTY MEMBER
INDIANA UNIVERSITY MAURER SCHOOL OF LAW
CBS RADIO HOST – *CAREER COACH CAROLINE*, AUTHOR
OF *THIS IS NOT THE CAREER I ORDERED*

"Want to give the perfect gift to a recent graduate about to enter the job market? Nancy Fox's *Network Like A Fox* will show them exactly what they need to do to meet the right people in the right places, how to network and build successful business relationships that will serve them throughout their career. (Of course it is a great gift for someone already IN the workplace too.)"

—Bob Siegal
Director, Management Advisory Services at Prager and Fenton Certified Public Accountants

"As a 'professional networker' and regional director of development for the preeminent professional networking organization in California, I observe many professional service providers and business owners trying to figure out how to develop relationships with the right people. This isn't something that they've ever been taught, and too often it's hit or miss, without any real strategy. *Network Like A Fox* addresses this issue head on and offers a bulls eye approach to strategic networking. It's highly recommended reading for all savvy business people who want to be more successful at business building through relationship building."

—Deborah Rodney,
Regional Director of Development for ProVisors

"I've helped many clients network with the media and *Network Like A Fox* introduces key concepts that can help you meet the right people at the right places faster and more effectively so you get better results.

You can spin your wheels networking in all the wrong places, or you can start to develop the right networking strategy for you and your business."

—Dan Janal, author "Reporters Are Looking for YOU!" and Founder of PRLEADS.com

"What a breath of fresh air! In this book, Nancy unpacks the secrets to successful and meaningful networking. She provides a systematic, targeted approach to cultivating the right business relationships to help you win. Irrespective of work experience, *Network Like A Fox* is an essential tool for anyone who wants to get more bang for their networking buck."

—IAIN WORSLEY, SENIOR VICE PRESIDENT, PROFESSIONAL
SERVICES TEAM, CAPITAL ONE BANK

"When we reach out and take risks to network we create a connectedness that yields limitless opportunity — *Network Like A Fox* drives this message and provides important "how to" tenets. Reading *Network Like A Fox* will transform your personal power and influence to benefit you and your organization."

—CATHERINE HOLTZ
DIRECTOR, MARKETING
BAYER HEALTHCARE

"This is not just another book of networking tips. In *Network Like A Fox*, Nancy Fox has shared a unique approach for connecting wisely and successfully. Now you can learn how to get great results and build the right relationships in a fraction of the time. I've watched Nancy in action and she's the real deal. This is a must read if you want to meet the right people and gain their attention, trust, and their business."

—DAVID SCHNURMAN, CEO, FURTHERED.COM

"As a business owner and investor, networking is absolutely essential to my continued success — and much of what I learned, Nancy taught me. Her new book, *Network Like A Fox*, distills her wisdom into important lessons that make it easy for anyone to learn this critical skill and apply it to any situation, personal or professional. Do yourself a favor and take Nancy's advice by hanging out with the right people — the influencers, decision-makers, and connectors who can help you reach your goals — and start by hanging out with Nancy for a few hours, reading her book and absorbing her teachings."

—Tony Coretto, Co-CEO, PNT Marketing Services, Inc. (4-time Inc5000 company)

"I met Nancy at one of her amazing networking events. She quickly taught me the value of being in 'the right room, with the right people.' Nancy has worked with many of my clients and has helped them grow not only the caliber of their networks, but their top-line revenue and per partner net income. Read *Network Like A Fox* to learn to network in ways that produce tangible results."

—Philip Whitman CPA Partner, Erickson Whitman LLC

NETWORK LIKE A FOX

A TARGETED APPROACH

TO BUILDING SUCCESSFUL BUSINESS
RELATIONSHIPS, IN PERSON AND ONLINE

NANCY FOX

For information about this title or to order other books and/or electronic
media, contact the publisher:
Publishing Directions
P. O. Box 715
Avon, CT 06001
860 675-1344

Library of Congress Control Number: 2013937331

ISBN: 978-1-928782-44-5

Printed in the United States of America

Cover and Interior design by: 1106 Design

Contents

Acknowledgements

FOR YEARS, I've been fascinated with the topic of networking and how some people managed to meet the right people.

How do they do that? I wondered.

I became an avid networker to gain the answers and to be more successful in my business.

I also became ever more fascinated with this topic.

Then, in 2009, I made a decision to write this book and actually completed about 4 chapters.

But the world turned, the economy went into the tank, and my life and my ideas for my business changed significantly.

I was now too busy to write the book. It sat in my computer.

Late in 2011, I was feeling a bit bored and directionless and my friend Susan looked around my house and saw the old watercolors I had painted 20 years ago, the photographs I had snapped 15 years ago and asked me what I was doing these days to express my creativity.

I looked at her blankly.

Not much, I said.

Susan (bless her for her intuition) said, "You need to get back to working your right brain again, and get creative."

So I did.

I whipped out my digital camera and started taking black and whites again. I started painting furniture.

And then I remembered this book on networking sitting in my computer.

My mind was made up in that moment.

Now was the time. I was going to finish the book by December 31.

It was an amazing process — to put a stake in the sand and see a project through as planned.

But here's the creative surprise.

If I had completed the book in 2009, the breadth of ideas and projects that were now flowing out of me as a result of writing the book would never have emerged.

The timing wasn't right then. It was completely right now.

I have quite a few acknowledgements to make. I'm sure I'll think of dozens more after I release this manuscript to the editor but I will just have to live with that.

First, I want to thank my Dad for giving me the persistence lesson. I got all my determination, drive and unstoppability from him. Thank you, Dad, for teaching me those things. They have served me well.

I want to thank my BFF Liz Kallen for being my very first networking teacher. Thank goodness you had Tom Brokaw in your Palm Pilot, Lizzie. You inspired me from that moment forward, and you mentored me in more ways than you can ever know.

I want to thank my wonderful friend, Susan Rosenthal, for being so much smarter than I. You saw that while we started out as networking colleagues we really belonged in the great friend category. You make me feel lucky to have you for my friend.

I want to thank Alan Collins who in one short sentence gave me the key to believing I have what it takes.

I want to thank Suzanne Evans for being a brilliant namer. You are truly gifted and The Business Fox and Network Like A Fox wouldn't exist without your brilliance.

Thank you Josh for always having my back.

I want to thank all of the interviewees who generously allowed me to share your stories. I have learned from you, been inspired by you, and really enjoyed connecting with you.

And finally and most of all, I want to thank my sisters, Miriam and Judee.

My love for you and gratitude for having your support and love is beyond words.

Introduction

All Networking Is Not Created Equal.
—Nancy Fox

I LOVE networking.

Please don't stop reading in disgust. I didn't always feel this way.

I am not a natural extrovert, so talking to strangers does not come easily to me.

I am inherently nervous when speaking to people in positions of power and influence.

I don't have an MBA or a degree from a fancy college.

What I do have is the willingness and perseverance to do the "difficult" and often highly uncomfortable things in order to be successful. But I am not writing this book to tell you to do those difficult things. All the other books on networking have told you that already.

What I have learned is the underlying clue to success in business and in life.

And I've acquired this knowledge the hard way — by falling down a lot, making a lot of embarrassing mistakes, taking chances, and most of all by learning from those who are true masters at the game of business.

After three decades in business, both within the corporate world and in my own business, I've found ways to make networking, an absolute essential element for business success, fun, easy, and time-effective.

Over the years I have read dozens of books on networking. I'm betting you have read a lot of them too. Some of them are really excellent. Many of my favorites will be listed for you at the end of this book in my reading list. Some of those books sugarcoat networking by calling it some cutesy name to make it more palatable. But here's the deal: networking, by any name, and the process of networking, can instantly send shivers of fear through many a brilliant business person's body. The mere thought of walking into a room full of strangers, all in the hope of finding and obtaining new business or a new job, makes many people's stomachs do somersaults.

It's understandable but not excusable. Avoiding networking is not an option if you want to be successful.

What is an option is HOW you network and with WHOM you network. Why make it harder, longer, and more painful when you don't have to?

I am writing this book because after years of studying networking methods, and gathering thousands of business cards, I've learned some essential "secrets" to networking that result in both success and comfort with the process.

I'm going to give them to you in one line. Here are the keys to the kingdom:

Who you are is who you hang around with.

That's right. It's not about how many people are in your Rolodex. (OK, iPhone, Blackberry, or Samsung).

It's about whether or not the RIGHT people are in your Rolodex, iPhone or Blackberry.

Are they influencers? Are they decision makers? Are they connectors? Can the people in your Outlook list sign a check to give you the business? Can they introduce you to those people? Are they leaders and business generators? The next key to this revelation: Will these influencers, decision makers, and connectors take your calls? Will they introduce you to more influencers and decision makers because they know, like, and trust you? Are the people in your contact base at the right stature and level for your target market? Are they even in your target market, or do you have a contact base filled with yoga instructors when your business is software solutions for corporations?

I urge you to stop wasting your time meeting the wrong people, the people who will definitely waste your time. They will drain you and leave you feeling depleted, frustrated, and unsuccessful, and probably bored to tears.

You can build a better quality network, so that *a better quality of business opportunity* comes your way more quickly, so that you have more fun in the process, and best of all, so that you generate a better quality of relationships to boot.

I want to talk to you about how to upgrade your network, meet the right people, and get better results more easily and faster. That alone takes 50% of the problem out of networking. The other 50% will be addressed by helping you create a networking blueprint that suits you best. Who says you have to network in giant rooms with masses of strangers, trying to juggle a drink in one hand and a business card in the other? That might be OK if you like big groups of people. But if you don't, and you are more confident and effective with small groups or one-on-one, there are scores of other ways to build a burgeoning network filled with great people who are really up to something and where everyone benefits. You don't have to be the life of the party to succeed.

I want to help you devise some targeted networking methods that are not madness, that really allow you to meet people who fit your business objectives and model.

Once that happens, you start creating business opportunities with people who are in alignment with your values and objectives and you can start kicking some business ass. Maybe you even start having some fun!

Network Like A Fox™ is founded on some very specific tenets, tenets that most networking books don't address. They are the result of many years of trial and error, and I believe they are the source of business success.

Tenet 1: All Networking Is Not Created Equal

You can invest many hours, business cards, and dollars networking your butt off. If you don't situate yourself with the right populations and engage in effective follow-up activities, it's all a waste of time and effort.

Tenet 2. Your Attitude Is Your Aptitude

If you hate networking and approach it with this attitude, I'd advise you to forget it. Don't bother. Networking is just an extension of your interest and curiosity about people, what they are up to in business, and how you can help each other. It is not about going to networking events and expecting results quickly or immediately. It is a process and it is about your attitude toward and about other people.

Tenet 3. Who You Are Is Who You Hang Around With

Bottom line — if you hang around with successful people, statistics have proven your chances for success are magnified many times. Hang around with mediocre or negative people, and the converse is true.

Tenet 4. The Right Relationships = Real Business

People bandy the word "relationship" around without thinking about what it really means. A relationship is something that is generated when you relate to and with someone — i.e., you are interested in that person, what he or she is working on, whom they'd like to meet, what their business entails and who it serves. When relationships develop between people of like-minded interests and connections, between people who are of the same caliber of professionalism, tremendous opportunities start opening up for both people in the relationship.

Tenet 5. Networking Does Not Equal New Business. It Is Only The Plus Sign.

This is a very important tenet. People believe that if they begin to network that it should automatically bring them new business. Not so. Networking is a process that substantially increases the possibilities for new business. It works if you work it correctly. Therefore, I say it is the plus sign in the equation of success.

Desire + Attitude + The Right Network = Success

What will you learn by reading Network Like A Fox?:

- ► Specific ways to get out of your comfort zone and increase motivation to network properly.
- ► How to create a viable, successful networking strategy —locate which networking groups and events are right for you and your business or career.
- ► How to get involved and noticed in the right networks — how to build your memorable personal brand and increase your visibility in your network.
- ► How to meet and talk to decision makers.
- ► How to overcome any obstacles you encounter in your networking activities — to build your self confidence once and for all.
- ► Learn why you are networking your butt off and still not getting the business — what's in the way?
- ► How to network internally in your own company or firm to get noticed and get promoted.

- ▸ How networking online differs from networking in person, and the right ways to build relationships online.
- ▸ Learn a system for foolproof follow-up after the networking event is over.
- ▸ Success Stories: Case Studies of people who have used targeted networking and won in business and life.
- ▸ Some tools to use in learning how you can "network like a fox" and generate results with greater ease and speed.

Are you ready for a fresh new approach to networking, one that is targeted and relevant just for your personality and your business?

All right then, let's get started.

CHAPTER 1

Why Networking Is Making You Tired, Fatter, And Not Any Richer

A man wrapped up in himself makes a very small bundle.
—Benjamin Franklin

DURING MY TWO-DECADE corporate career, I occasionally attended industry networking events. They would usually be big rubber-chicken events, where I pretty much knew everyone and (after 20 years) they knew me. These networking events would be more important to me during times I was interested in making a job change, and of no interest at all when I wasn't. This probably sounds familiar to many of you.

When I launched my coaching and consulting business, I was faced with an astounding realization: I didn't have any contacts or relationships outside of my former industry. And my former industry (the women's intimate apparel field) didn't really embrace professional development or coaching. I suddenly became aware of the fact that I had a big problem.

For me, necessity became the mother of intervention. I got my butt out there and started networking — everywhere. Now I had two problems: I was networking in a less-than-robust business geographical area and I didn't know what I was doing.

After networking for nine months in a county that I found to be small-minded, and failing to find the kind of clients I wanted to work with, I had an epiphany: Just because I lived in that county didn't mean I should be networking in it. Duh!

Fortunately, I lived near New York City. Although it took greater effort, time, and sometimes money, I began attending events in NYC. Almost immediately, I felt the difference in energy and level of business assertiveness. People were up to things, they were interested in new ideas, working on new projects. People were in action. The people I was meeting were often running businesses that were significantly larger than those I had been contacting in my home county.

While this was definitely an improvement, it still didn't address my main interest, which was to meet the people who were the decision makers of companies and firms who could hire me. Now this goes against all that I teach about building relationships, and that networking isn't about me, it's about you. That is true. But at the end of the day, I am much more interesting to other people when my network is of greater influence. I will talk more about building relationships and expectations around networking in Chapter 5.

What happened was a stroke of luck. But that stroke of luck was not just a business stroke of luck. It was an aha! stroke of luck, meaning I had a huge awareness of how meeting the right people positively influences your business results.

Around this time, a new Whole Foods opened in Edgewater, New Jersey. For those of you who don't know this area of the country, Edgewater is a very affluent area. Many top-level executives live there because it faces the Hudson River and is in close proximity to NYC. Whole Foods was just entering the New Jersey market and they launched a calendar of classes and seminars and were looking for speakers. I happened to be in Whole Foods, met the new marketing director, got her card, and reached out to her. She happened to be intrigued by this new profession she had been hearing about, coaching, and immediately put me on the regular monthly schedule for courses at Whole Foods.

At first, I thought it was a waste of time. Classes were small, attendance irregular. However, during the six months of classes I led at Whole Foods, I was hired by two major corporations through attendees of my classes referring me into their companies. In each of these cases, those assignments lasted for several years (!). How did this happen?

The people attending these classes were people in positions of influence in viable companies who had the interest, the ability, and the readiness to engage professional development consultants. And this didn't occur during a particularly strong economic period. We all remember the time right after 9/11 as a time of business stagnation and fear. Yet, the right people in the right positions in the right companies were influential, and were willing and able to lead me to the right decision makers.

We could say I got lucky. Yes, there was some luck involved. But I don't think it was accidental that in two cases, in Edgewater, New Jersey, I met people with access to and influence with decision makers. It's more likely that Edgewater is a hub of influencers. And influencers are often interested in learning and professional development. Whole Foods is an upscale gourmet food retailer, so it attracted a more upscale customer. While not everyone that shops at Whole Foods is an influential upscale executive or business owner, Whole Foods often draws customers from a certain demographic. I landed in the middle of opportunity and it paid off.

What I find most people do when they network is network in all the places that feel more comfortable to them.

Lawyers network within bar associations. Accountants network with other accountants.

Start-up business owners attend networking groups with other start-up businesses.

People tend to network where it feels easy and safe.

This is exactly the strategy that will delay your business success and leave you wondering what all the hooplah about networking is about.

When I was a little girl, my father told me that I should always make friends with people who were smarter, more successful, and better educated than I. While, as most kids do, I usually dismissed parental advice as worthless and antiquated, I knew as soon as he had imparted this to me the wisdom in it. I absorbed this input right into my pores, intuitively realizing how valuable it was.

We have all received similar input growing up. What did our parents tell us as kids?

If you hang around with the good kids, you'll have a good life.

If you hang around with the bad kids...

The problem is we tend to gravitate to what feels comfortable and easy. But comfortable and "easy" is not where your target market is hanging out. It is much easier to engage in conversations with people who are at our level, in our field, with whom we feel similar and more confident. It's much more challenging and uncomfortable to attempt to have conversation with people who are in positions more senior to us, or who hold influence with companies we'd like to work in or with.

Right there is the crux of the networking problem.

If you network with people who are easy and safe, your business results generally will take longer to produce. The people who are easiest and safest to build relationships with often don't have the influence or decision-making power to make a difference in your business. And even more importantly, by filling your network with people who don't have much influence, you have less impact with other business people.

If your contacts include decision makers and influential business people, you immediately have more credibility because you have the ability to introduce higher-level people to new contacts.

By becoming a connector of more established and successful business people, your value in the marketplace is elevated. Therefore, networking in less comfortable venues, where you are interacting with leaders and influencers, will allow you to develop higher quality business opportunities as well as increasing your credibility and value in the marketplace as a connector.

There are three reasons people take the safe, easy route in networking:

1. They are scared of talking to more influential people.
2. They are scared that the decision makers they meet will reject them or say no.
3. They are scared they will look foolish or stupid with those more accomplished or with those who hold the power to give them business or hire them.

Let's take a minute to look at how people actually work networking:

A client of mine (let's call him Joe) is a brilliant lawyer. Joe is also one of the nicest guys I know. Joe really wants to develop business and has been unable to do so, no matter how much he networks. I asked him for some details about the people he knows, who he hangs around with, professionally and personally, and where he's been networking.

Joe and his wife live in an affluent area, his neighbors and friends are quite successful, and he and his wife play tennis with top executives and business owners. His children go to school with children of many successful professionals and business people.

He has never been hired by any of these folks. Nor has he ever been given a referral by any of these people.

I asked him to tell me about the relationships he has with these people, and to tell me what they talk about. I also asked him where he networks.

Joe tells me he is "uncomfortable" talking about business with these folks. He is concerned they will think he is selling them.

Joe decided he needed to join a networking group. He found a group that meets once a week at 7 AM. In order to get to these meetings on time, Joe has to get up at 4 AM. What's been the outcome of his efforts? Who has he been meeting? Start-up businesses and small business owners, very few of whom can afford his legal services. In the last several months, Joe has referred business to three of his fellow networking members. He's received one referral, to a company who would love to work with Joe but can't afford him.

Another colleague of mine, Sally, began her career as an executive assistant to very successful business people. She wanted more, went back to school at night and got her master's degree, and finally was ready to compete for a much bigger job. She also needed a much bigger paycheck as she is the primary breadwinner in her family. Leveraging some of her contacts in her search for a higher paying position, she landed an interview in a small business poised for growth. Sally had the drive and the smarts, but it was a new business sector for her. She landed the job as head of business development.

As head of business development, her charge was to bring new business to the table. Sally started networking non-stop. After 6 months she had hundreds of business cards. She accepted every invitation to every networking event extended to her. After all that time, she was exhausted, had gained 15 pounds from all the breakfasts, lunches and dinners, and had not closed a single deal. Her boss was getting nervous and so was Sally. That's when Sally asked me to help her.

We talked about the people she was meeting. Then we talked about who her ideal referral partners would be. I immediately saw a big disconnect. She was meeting lots of small entrepreneurs. Who did she need to be meeting? The most likely attorneys who would refer business to her were trust and estate attorneys. These professionals were the people who could actually decide to engage her. We did some research as to where these attorneys were congregating. What associations did they belong to? Where were they speaking? Which firms specialized in this category?

Sally started to network almost exclusively with these attorneys. In the next few months, every attorney in this specialization in her city knew her. How did this happen? She had breakfast and lunch every day with different lawyers, built a robust, targeted, contact base, and soon had booked over $100K in new business. The following year, she was invited to speak at industry conferences.

That's what targeted networking can do for your business.

Keith Ferrazzi, in his best-selling book, *Never Eat Alone,* shares his personal rags-to-networking riches success story. His father, a blue-collar worker, courageously went to the owner of the company he worked for (a Yale University alumna) to ask for a recommendation to Yale University for his son. He knew that his son's chances of success were exponentially expanded by living amongst the best and brightest for the next four years. The brave request paid off. Keith graduated from Yale University. Keith applied what he learned from this experience by ultimately becoming the youngest Chief Marketing Officer at Deloitte Consulting. He had learned to connect and develop positive relationships with leaders and influencers in his company.

Let's analyze the results of these three case studies.

Joe's lack of business success can be traced directly to taking the safe, easy route in networking:

1. He is frightened and uncomfortable interacting with more influential people so he selected a networking group that was

much more difficult to attend just so that he could network with less-threatening people.

2. He hasn't discussed business with friends and contacts he's known for years for fear they will reject him. When he has discussed business, he reflects a lack of confidence, so they don't feel confident referring business to him. A real Catch 22. It becomes a self-fulfilling prophecy.

3. Joe is concerned he will look foolish by discussing business with successful business people. He's concerned he will sound like a salesperson, so he avoids these conversations.

By contrast, Sally put a pause button on things when she saw them not working. She rethought the situation and created a new strategy. She was willing to organize her time and efforts and get involved in the right networking arena. Disregarding fear and discomfort, she started to attend events that attracted her ideal referral partners. Sally started to develop relationships with them, meeting with them, introducing them to some of the business people she knew (potential clients for them). She refused to focus on any fear or lack of confidence and replaced it with desire to be of service and value to these potential clients. She continually expressed genuine interest in their business.

Keith consciously leveraged relationships and opportunities developed through his education at Yale. Once he graduated, he was recruited to work at Deloitte. Using the same relationship-building principles, and despite the fact that he was young and inexperienced, he learned to connect with and interact with influencers in his firm, including the CEO. This allowed him to gain exposure to the inner workings of the firm and determine how he might best contribute in meaningful ways.

In each of these scenarios, there were roadblocks to break through. Next, let's look at how to overcome these roadblocks.

CHAPTER 2

Breaking Through Those Big Networking Roadblocks

*I've come to believe that all my past failure and frustration
were actually laying the foundation for the understandings
that have created the new level of living I now enjoy.*
—Tony Robbins

Your networking roadblocks can be overcome — if you are
willing to learn some completely new approaches to meeting and
connecting with people.

Most people get seriously stopped in their networking results due
to what I call networking-itis — the fear of networking:

The good news is there are some really tangible antidotes to this
fear — six of them.

1. preparation
2. research
3. asking excellent open-ended questions
4. listening

5. curiosity and interest in others
6. Leaping in — the water's fine

How most people approach their networking efforts is the "hit and miss method."

This method usually goes something like this:

You hear about a networking group from a friend or colleague. You join the group.

After several months of early morning meetings and lots of breakfasts and lunches, you're fatter, frustrated and disappointed because you haven't generated business from this or that networking group, or maybe you've gotten some small pieces of business but nothing like the caliber of client you had in mind when you joined. It can be disheartening.

I want to share a case study of a young man who applied the 6 antidotes to networking-itis, who "networked like a fox" for his business and came out a big winner — and so did the firm he worked for.

Brian is a young professional in his late twenties. He is a reasonably good technician in his field of accounting; he's well educated and bright. But what sets Brian apart from the pack is his huge drive. Brian has a very big **why** for becoming successful. He comes from a family of successful entrepreneurial siblings, and this has motivated Brian in a big way. Normally, in his firm, it would take about ten years to make partner. This didn't seem very appealing to Brian. His biggest desire was not so much to be made partner but to become a successful, well-connected business consultant and well-compensated rainmaker.

So often this is not encouraged in professional service firms. Professional service firms prefer their younger employees to start slow, learn the technical aspects of the profession, and slowly advance along the pathway to partnership.

Brian decided not to let his age, inexperience, or the opinions of naysayers get in his way.

First, he selected business arenas that he felt were growing and that interested him. The niches he chose were hedge funds and real estate. Let's continue to see how these choices played out for him.

Brian began by networking everywhere (similar to Sally). He also started his own networking group. After several months of some pretty disappointing results and mediocre relationships, he tweaked his strategies. His networking group wasn't high level enough for him, so he turned the reins over to one of the other members. He started to hone where he was networking. He began attending hedge fund presentations and seminars, a direct connection into the industry he wanted to penetrate.

At one of these seminars, he boldly (some might say brazenly) walked up to the Managing Director of a real estate hedge fund, introduced himself (he mentioned his firm but not his title) and asked if he might attend the next presentation and bring several business colleagues who might be potential investors. He had been carefully gathering the business cards of higher net worth individuals for a while, and here was his opportunity to connect them with opportunity and a higher caliber network. At the next meeting, Brian showed up with nine guests. Do you think the Managing Director of the real estate hedge fund took notice?

What transpired over the next several months was a series of meetings between Brian and the management of the hedge fund. It turned out that the fund was exploring changing accounting firms and was interviewing potential candidates. Brian got a lot of background information by asking why they were making a change and what their specific needs and interests were. He went back to his own firm and did some research and preparation about the full capabilities of the firm. Then he circled back to the hedge fund, suggesting they should meet the management of his firm as a possible candidate. The hedge fund actually was a conglomerate of hedge funds, so the new service firm would not be winning one client, but an entire group of clients and projects. Brian initiated the pitch to this hedge fund and after four months of meetings between his firm's partners and those of the hedge fund, Brian landed the client.

At the age of 29, Brian brought in the single largest new client in the history of his firm, a deal in the neighborhood of seven figures. This landed Brian two promotions in two consecutive years. The firm made him a partner in his sixth year at the firm.

To many of Brian's peers in the firm, Brian's actions were overly confident. To others, it was difficult to grasp how at his age and level of experience, he could connect with such high-level business people and bring this deal to fruition.

To be sure, Brian had an enormous amount of guidance and assistance from his firm's leaders. He could not have closed the deal effectively without them. But here's what Brian did to make it possible to seal the deal:

- ▶ Preparation — Brian prepared himself about the leaders of the hedge fund before attending the seminars.
- ▶ Research — Brian did some background research about the company on the Internet and through contacts in his network.
- ▶ Asked excellent questions — At the seminars, Brian asked the Managing Director and other leaders about their objectives, challenges, and ideal investor candidates.
- ▶ Listening — Brian listened carefully to what they were looking for AND he listened for opportunity. When they expressed their business concerns and dissatisfactions he knew this was an opportunity to provide them with better solutions.
- ▶ Curiosity and interest in others — Brian didn't pitch them too soon; he expressed interest in their business and how he could be helpful to them. He walked his talk by bringing new relationships and potential investors to their presentations. Nothing is more important to business people who are hosting events than filling the room with quality people. Brian

came through with good people. After he had demonstrated his interest in helping them and their business, the hedge fund leaders were more open to hearing Brian's suggestion to consider his firm as a potential candidate.

▸ Leap in: The water's fine — Brian took a chance and didn't let his concern about his youth (most young professionals don't feel competent, confident, or knowledgeable enough to interact with decision makers and leaders) prevent him from introducing himself to the decision makers of the hedge fund.

The point should now be clear: You can spin your wheels networking in all the wrong places, or you can start to develop a targeted networking strategy for you and your business.

In order to get where you want to go, you need to know where you are going.

This seems ridiculously obvious, right? It's stunning how many people have no idea about specifically who they'd like to be networking with.

In order to develop your targeted networking strategy, you need to know who you want to meet.

That's exactly what's up next: How to determine the right networking groups and venues for you and your business.

CHAPTER 3

How To Find The Right Networking Groups And Events For You

Fear isn't an excuse to come to a standstill.
It's the impetus to step up and strike.
—Arthur Ashe

Now that you see the value of targeted networking, interacting in the right places with the right people, you're faced with determining:

Who should you be networking with?

How do you find them?

How do you integrate into these networks?

How do you build relationships with these folks?

First, it is essential to understand that your ideal network, your "sweet spot" network, is actually broken down into Four Connection Archetypes:

Ideal *Prospects* — these are the perfect potential clients or customers for you, ones who will allow you to **build your business with ease.**

Ideal *Introducers* (**Connectors**) — People in your network who are highly connected to many influencers and decision makers and who will introduce you to other high quality influencers and decision makers in their network.

Ideal *Referrers* — People who understand you and your business, are thinking of you as a resource for people they know, **and actually send potential clients your way.**

Ideal "**sweet spot**" *Clients* (**end users**) — Your clients are often the best and richest resource for new connections and prospects.

Your "sweet spot" network, where all four of the **ideal** archetypes are found, is what I call your "Grow Zone."

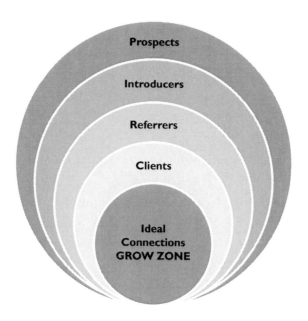

Your "Grow Zone" is the richest, most productive, and most rewarding world of connections. This is the heart of what will make your world really come alive, not just suffice.

As we explore what your targeted networking strategy should be, and who you should be meeting, and as you begin networking with greater awareness and intention, you will automatically begin to consciously slot your new contacts into archetype categories. Sometimes, a connection will fall into more than one category. But it will become more and more clear into which domain they fall, making it easier for you to determine which people you should prioritize in building relationships, and who are not as critical in the overall picture.

By breaking your network down into four main archetypes, it becomes easier to create a smart networking strategy and gauge with whom to spend more time and how to bring yourself into proximity with your ideal people.

One of the best examples of someone who has applied strategic networking and achieved outstanding results is Mike Michalowicz. Mike is a super-successful entrepreneur and a multiple-time best-selling author. He's built several businesses, going beyond the million dollar mark more than once. Read on for a great story about how Mike and his networking strategies have paid off handsomely:

CASE STUDY
Mike Michalowicz
Serial Entrepreneur, Best-selling Author of
"The Toilet Paper Entrepreneur"

Mike Michalowicz is one of the smartest and most successful entrepreneurs out there. He has launched and sold 2 multi-million dollar companies, and currently operates his third, Obsidian Launch, a consulting firm that ignites explosive growth in companies that have plateaued. And he's the author of not one, but two best-selling business books, The Toilet Paper Entrepreneur, and The Pumpkin Plan. He is also a former columnist for The Wall Street Journal and the host for the business makeover segment on MSNBC's weekly show "Your Business". That gives you a snapshot of Mike's business cred.

When it comes to networking, most of us think about growing new contacts and relationships by going "out there" and networking.

Mike thinks differently. He asked himself, "What is already within my environment that I can leverage?"

Watch this:

Mike's technology consulting business was thriving. One key strategy that led to the explosive growth of his original company, Olmec, was through "nicheing up." Mike realized that 30 percent of Olmec's annual revenue was coming from hedge fund firms, but they had only a handful of hedge fund clients. So a big lightbulb went on over Mike's head. He said: How can we capture more business within this niche and own it?

Obviously a specialization in hedge fund clients meant marketing to more of these kinds of firms.

The challenge: how to meet more decision makers in this niche?

The strategy Mike employed was to ask his hedge fund clients not to introduce him to other hedge fund leaders (that would have been uncomfortable for his clients), but to introduce him to their other vendors.

Why would they want to do this? What's in it for them? Because Mike understands how people think, he knows what will ring their bell.

Mike explains to his top clients he wants to better serve them, the client, by understanding and forming integrative support along with the other vendors. This is not just lip service on Mike's part. This really is part of his nature — support his clients to the nth degree.

Totally unique approach, right?

One of Mike's hedge fund clients was so impressed with this desire to go the extra step to better serve them he handed Mike a list of 5 vendors and the names of his main contact at each company.

Then Mike took it a strategic step further: He asked his client which vendor they depended on the most.

As his client mentioned their top vendor, Mike asked if he'd mind if he spoke with the vendor and tell them what they'd been discussing.

Mike got the green light, contacted the leader at the key vendor, Ben, and explained he had been referred by their mutual client. His purpose was to get Ben's advice on how Mike could be working to make the vendor's job easier in servicing their mutual client, and how they both could do a better job for their mutual client.

In the end, Mike's conversation with Ben led to a growing, thriving relationship with Ben and the vendor company. As that relationship deepened, Mike earned Ben's confidence and trust which ultimately led to Ben introducing Mike to several other hedge fund companies.

Mike's networking approach shows a really savvy understanding about how to build niche-dominance, and do it through opening up rich, high-potential connections that exist right in your own client backyard.

(You can read more of this story and other fantastic strategies in Mike's book, www.thepumpkinplan.com, The Pumpkin Plan, Portfolio/Penguin, ©2012)

Where Will Your "Sweet Spot" Network Be Hanging Out?

The questions people ask me most frequently about networking is, "How do I find the right people?" and "How do I figure out where to go to meet them?"

In order to determine the best places frequented by your ideal network, you must put yourself in your target audience's shoes. They say that in order to step into someone else's shoes, you need to first take off your own. Truer words were never spoken. You must take the time to step out of your own mindset, and think the way your target network thinks.

I am amazed at how much people talk about wanting to be successful, yet they do not invest any time in thinking about what they are doing, what they should be doing. They just do. To connect in the right places with the right people, it is going to take some think time about what your ideal market is dealing with, interested in, attracted to, worried about. When you have a sense of the answers to these questions, you will learn where they are hanging out.

And how do you begin to think like someone else thinks?

The best way to learn how your ideal target network thinks is by asking some questions.

Have you ever asked your clients or prospective clients where they network or what associations they belong to?

When I ask my clients this question, I usually get the 'deer in the headlights" reaction.

I encourage you to ask every client or valued contact you have in your database these questions:

"I am interested in raising the bar on my networking activities. Where do you network? What associations do you belong to and participate in? What organizations do you participate in and why do you like them? Which ones don't you recommend?"

To research the right networking venues, I like to break the process down and examine these event categories:

- ► Industry and professional associations and their events
- ► General business organizations and associations
- ► Educational conferences — often generated and hosted by industry associations
- ► Chambers of Commerce, Rotary Clubs, local business centers
- ► Private networking groups
- ► Non-profit activities and fundraisers
- ► Trade and other publications — What is your target audience reading? (announcements of associations and groups will be posted in these publications and advertised there)

Within these categories, you will find various demographics of participants. For example, general educational conferences will attract a cross section of attendees. However, if, for example, we look at Harvard Business School's Advanced Management Program: Transforming Proven Leaders into Global Executives, during which global leaders spend eight transformative weeks stepping back to re-examine the way they think, manage, and solve problems, at a cost of $60,000, we know that this educational conference will clearly attract a high-level, highly influential, successful group of people. If your position or business calls for you to be attracting global leaders and decision makers, this would be a plum place to connect with them. And, although the price tag is $60,000, you will be interacting with this ideal population and creating deep-seeded bonds with these folks over the course of eight weeks. This investment would not only result in a higher level of knowledge, but integrates you into an incredible network of influencers and decision makers.

Consider this: if just one of those connections results in a six-figure business deal, wouldn't the return on such an investment be well worth it? And not only that, consider too the future opportunities. Priceless.

This course will also very likely have alumni activities and events so the benefits of this educational investment is the kind of investment that keeps on giving.

In this example of attending educational conferences, I've used a very high-end example here to illustrate how you might select an educational conference and get massive payback in your network-building benefits.

The Internet is a wealth of up-to-date information if you use it strategically. By Googling through LinkedIn searches you can glean enormous amounts of information about where people are congregating.

An excellent resource for learning more about how to connect with the affluent is Dr. Thomas J. Stanley's book, *Networking With The Affluent*. Dr. Stanley also wrote the best-selling book, *The Millionaire Next Door.*

Who do the affluent interact with? Using some connect-the-dots logic, here are some likely places they are congregating:
- Charitable fundraisers
- Speaking at high-level conferences
- Country clubs, golf and tennis events
- High end resorts
- First class seats on airplanes or private jets

Who do the affluent seek as their advisors?
- Financial advisors
- Corporate attorneys
- CPAs
- Business brokers
- Insurance advisors

Who else would the affluent be interacting with?

- ▸ Luxury product sales — auto, jewelry, private jets, etc.
- ▸ Family office managers
- ▸ Board members of non-profits (often senior executives and successful business owners)
- ▸ Other affluent parents watching their kids on the soccer field
- ▸ Ski resorts and other high-priced vacation spots

Knowing where the affluent are congregating is the first step in connecting with them.

Then, it's all about putting yourself in the environments where they are.

I recently read about a resourceful, determined business owner buying a first class airline ticket from New York to Los Angeles. He had learned that an ideal prospect was to be on that flight and that this prospect always flew first class. He purchased the seat next to this prospect, and had 6 hours to start a conversation, build rapport, and open the door to an ideal opportunity. That first class ticket was a small price to pay for a big business opportunity.

Put yourself where your "sweet spot" market is.

Now let's take a look at how you might access the right people in traditional networking groups.

Types Of Networking Groups: Which Are Right For You?

Millions of people join networking groups every year. The hope is that in those groups you will either meet your ideal prospective clients or people who will be able to refer business to you.

Finding the right networking group for you is essential to the outcomes for your business.

Most people select these groups based on recommendations from friends. Rarely are these decisions made strategically.

Your personality type and your level of networking experience impact the kind of networking events and groups in which you'll thrive.

I've separated business networking groups into three basic categories:

- **The Big "Rubber Chicken" Events:** Unstructured Networking
- **Structured Networking And Referral Groups:** Smaller Groups/Structured/Meet Regularly
- **Hybrid:** Some combination of the first two categories

The Big "Rubber Chicken" Events: Unstructured Networking

If you are a "people person" and have little or no qualms about mingling and working a room with a broader mix of people, bigger unstructured events are a good option for you. The benefit is that you get the chance to meet more people. The downside is you are left on your own to make ideal use of the time to meet and connect with ideal people. These kind of events, at best, will allow you to read the nametags of people so you can have a guide to chatting up ideal people.

On the downside, it is more difficult to navigate a big, unstructured room of people.

Sometimes the event organizers will publish a list of attendees/registrants before the event. When organizers do this, it's helpful because you can then prepare for whom you'd like to meet. A good idea is to contact the event organizers and ask for an introduction to your ideal contacts. Usually, they are eager to assist you so that you will have a favorable event experience.

Structured Networking And Referral Groups

For people who are newer to networking and are more comfortable in smaller groups, I recommend you begin honing your networking skills in smaller, structured networking groups.

There are usually dozens of these in every major city and even smaller towns, so figuring out which ones are right for you and your business is crucial. Remember the 6 antidotes to networking-itis? The most important one is to do your research. Do this before you join any group.

Normally, a networking group will allow you to attend one or more meetings before you join.

It is really important that you learn who the members are, what level of networking and connecting they are capable of, and most importantly, who are in the members' networks. If they don't have the kind of connections you are interested in, it will not be a fruitful experience no matter how comfortable you feel.

You want to know that the people you'll be networking with have access to the same kinds of people you want to be meeting. Sometimes these structured groups only allow one of each kind of business/service provider in the group to prevent conflicts of interest. Sometimes, a group will allow more than one specialist in the group.

If you are clear about your value proposition, having another similar member won't hurt you, and may even benefit you. After all, there is a lot of competition out there. You may as well craft a solid, clear competitive value proposition and message so people know exactly why they should recommend you as the go-to person in your business arena.

Some groups are solely focused on giving and getting referrals. This may feel a bit high-pressured for you. Other groups are more open minded and offer a combination of peer support and referrals.

Again, do your research and attend some meetings to see which groups are a good fit for you.

If you find yourself disliking going to your networking group every week or month, it will not very likely produce results for you and you won't be at your best for contributing to the group.

Hybrid Networking Groups

Sometimes networking groups offer some combination of the first two categories. There is some structure and some open-type of networking. As you get more solid in your networking approach and strategy, this may be a great option for you.

Bringing Your Ideal Network Into Your Own "Conference Room"

Going to networking events can often be a hit or miss proposition. How can you increase the odds for meeting the "right" people for your business on a regular basis?

Albert Einstein once said, "If we attempt to gain new insight on a problem, we cannot use old thinking."

Thus, if we keep trying to approach "meeting the right people" with an old approach, it is likely to produce similar results.

What if instead of being a networking attendee, you take a more proactive approach and you become the host to your GROW ZONE target audience?

By hosting your own networking events, consider these potential benefits:

- ▸ You are regarded as a thought leader
- ▸ You gain visibility
- ▸ You are meeting only the right people because you have hand-picked them
- ▸ You have direct access to all the "right people" attendees

Sounds great, right? OK, how do you make that happen? Filling the room with the right people is not so easy.

Or is it?

The thing to remember is that the people you want to meet will come to you **if you give them something they want**. I specifically did not say something they **need,** because people will act more out of want than need.

Here are three examples of successful business people who began bringing their target network into their own conference room and got lots of new business through that method.

A partner in a CPA firm specializes in staffing companies and restaurants. He and a colleague, who specializes in financing staffing companies, devised a way of collaborating and getting in front of ideal clients and prospects each month. Together they mapped out 10 key topics that leaders and CFO's of staffing companies would want to learn about.

Sometimes they would be the speakers on some of these topics; at other times, they invited other experts to speak on the other topics. Then, they pooled their contact lists and invited these leaders to monthly conference room roundtables 10 months out of the year. They hosted these lunchtime staffing roundtables for about 20–25 executives each month — and all it cost was the price of some sandwiches, soda, and cookies.

The benefits:

They were in front of their ideal network every month (so they remained uppermost in their minds). Often they were the featured speaker so attendees would come up to them afterward and ask them to help them with their business. They were regarded as thought leaders, built frequent touches and reminders in the minds of their ideal audience, and almost always got leads, referrals, and new business out of these inexpensive roundtable meetings. Plus they built additional referral sources through the other speakers they invited to address these groups.

A business development executive at another company decided to host Happy Hours every 60 days with her featured contacts. She would find reasonable locations, often donated, to host Happy Hours for about 20–30 of her key contacts. For a nominal investment, she was "top of mind" each month without being a pushy salesperson. Happy Hours were backed up by follow-up breakfasts to discuss specific opportunities with attendees. She brought her ideal network to her, and often created sub-groups by hosting real estate professionals one month, an entertainment group another month, etc.

A third colleague did something more extensive. He sponsored and hosted a monthly networking event for senior level professionals each month. The breakfast meetings were free for attendees, the events were by invitation only, and only targeted professionals who were interested in referring business to one another were invited.

Each month, about 70 attendees participated; there was a featured speaker and guests suggested new attendees.

New attendees had to be approved in order to keep the caliber of the group very high. Only certain targeted populations were invited. My colleague, as host, addressed and led the event each month, staying "top of mind" and developing relationships with attendees afterward. Since these events were held in official clubs, the price tag was higher, but the buzz it generated in the market was also higher.

These are three examples of how savvy and strategic business people brought the right networks into their own conference rooms.

Inviting People To The Right Events

It might be a challenge to get the right people in the room if you don't have the right people on your list.

A key solution that provides multiple benefits is to partner with other non-competitive business folks who are targeting the same population. Some examples might be:

Wedding planners and wedding dress retailers.
Target Attendees: Brides-to-be

Business Furniture Manufacturers and Architects.
Target Attendees: Facilities Managers, Commercial Interior
Design Firms

Commercial Real Estate Brokers, Real Estate Attorneys,
Accountants specializing in real estate.
Target Attendees: Real Estate Developers

By pooling your lists of possible attendees, you expand your reach
and share the financial and time requirements to host a breakfast
seminar or roundtable discussion event.

You've Identified The Right Places To Network — Now What?
Let's say you go the typical route and have decided to go to the right
events to build a better network. What's next?

Usually, when people figure out where they need to be networking in order to interact with the "right" people they begin to "attack"
their "victims" with pitches of their services or their products. Nothing
could be worse. I know: most of you think this doesn't apply to you.

I attended a conference with a client of mine. He is an experienced,
seasoned business advisor.

We were networking in the perfect environment for his area of
specialization. Business owners were everywhere at this event, and
he was the only specialist of his kind at the conference. We were at a
morning networking breakfast and I engaged a business owner in a
conversation. I introduced my client, who is a CPA, into the conversation. As he began speaking with this business owner, the first question
was "Who does your accounting currently?" You could literally see
the business owner physically leaning away from us. Unfortunately,
my client didn't see this at all. He launched into an entire disserta-
tion on how much experience he had with these kinds of businesses,

name-dropped a famous client, and went into a non-stop soliloquy that left both business owner and me bored to tears. He didn't ask a single question of his new contact. What a shame. The bigger shame is that this accountant, a partner in a successful firm, fancies himself a major networker and rainmaker. Well, to his credit, it was exactly why he hired me: to help him overcome his tendency to launch into non-stop talking and pitching people. This conversation certainly led to my having an eye-opening debrief conversation with my client.

I assure you, this kind of situation happens so often and most people have huge blind spots about their own networking and relationship-building actions. It's so easy for them to see this kind of networking turn-off in others, rarely in themselves.

So while determining the right places to network is an essential element in building the right network for your success, what you do once you get there is equally important.

The idea is for you to become a magnet for the right people and the right opportunities.

So how do you engage people in conversation with your ideal target audience, become a magnet and develop relationships, not come across as pushy or salesy, yet still get the message out that you are open for business?

The key is patience and consistency. You cannot develop a relationship in 10 minutes. In advertising, the rule of thumb is it takes seven touches or outreach messages for people to remember something about your brand or the product. In relationship development, the same requirement exists: It takes 5–7 times for people to see you, hear about you, or talk to you to get a sense of who you are, what you are about, and start feeling as though they are ready to build a relationship with you.

Sometimes The Right People Just Click!

A few years ago, I was researching a particular industry as an area for business opportunity — the entertainment industry. I asked a friend of mine if she knew anyone in the field. She didn't, but a friend of hers was involved with lots of people in that industry. I called him and he suggested I take a look at the Celebrity Professional Assistants Association.

That association has two branches, one on the West Coast and the other on the East Coast. I contacted the executive directors of both.

Someone from the NY Chapter returned my call that same day. On the phone, this woman and I immediately hit it off.

We met for coffee the next day. There was instant affinity between us. Our goals and values resonated with one another. We were both avid networkers and listed people we could introduce to one another.

My new colleague was a sales rep in a major bank; she was also looking for new job opportunities. She asked me to coach her on upcoming job interviews. I really saw a lot of potential in her and encouraged her to ask for a much higher salary than she was intending on negotiating for. She not only got the job, she got the bigger salary she had asked for. That launched us into becoming fast friends and we have been introducing people to one another ever since. This friendship has resulted in new clients for both of us, greater levels of visibility and success, and we've hosted events together that were both lucrative and fun.

Sometimes you just "click" with someone and it becomes a very fruitful and fun connection.

Introduce People To Each Other — But Don't Expect Anything In Return

If you start retraining your brain about becoming a connector, introducing the right people to one another, you will be astonished at how desirable, respected, and valued you become. Introducing the right people to each other also provides two very important things for you, in addition to enhancing your value and respect level:

> ▸ It demonstrates your generosity and your networking "get it" factor.

▸ It allows you to interact with your target network without asking for anything. This takes enormous pressure off of you and your contacts.

Many people would also add another advantage here. They would say this makes people beholden to you. While that may be true, I don't advise focusing on that. Focusing on a "tit for tat" and "I did this for you, now you owe me" attitude is very old school. It also generates an expectation within you that invariably will leave you disappointed and frustrated. Very often, we do things for others and don't get anything in return from that person.

A former client of mine is an active and generous networker. David has introduced many people to one another and helped many in his network. One day, David said to me, "You know, I am fuming. I have been helping one of the guys in my network group for months. I've been introducing him to great people and giving him referrals. I just heard that he recommended another company for an opportunity we would have been great for. What's up with people?"

I know David wasn't expecting my answer. I told him, "You're the problem here. You've been expecting something in return. I don't know why your network colleague referred someone over you. But your generosity will come back to you. However, it may not come back to you from the person you've been helping. And you've made a big mistake in the networking game: expecting anything from people is a setup for disappointment. People do the things they do, and sometimes we just can't figure out why."

Not expecting anything in return is very difficult for most people. It is one of the reasons people are so disgusted with networking. Yet, the solution to this is completely letting go of expectations. It is the way to set yourself free. If people don't return the favors you provide, don't get mad or disappointed. Get moving, meet more good people, sow more seeds. You will meet the right people who will definitely introduce you to good people. Your stress and frustration level will plummet.

CASE STUDY
Misty & Gary Young
Restaurateurs
Connecting with the Right People Led to a Recipe for Success at the Squeeze In Restaurant

Misty Young knows good people.

Filled with enthusiasm, energy, and a huge dose of "give to others" generosity, she naturally attracted the attention of superb leaders and influencers such as former Nevada Attorney General, Frankie Sue Del Papa.

In the early days of Misty's career, she and Del Papa were thrown together on the campaign trail when Misty was running a campaign. They bonded and eventually Del Papa recruited Misty to be her Press Secretary after the election.

This plum role put Misty in the midst of a powerful circle of political influencers and the media.

Misty's husband of 34 years, Gary, was a heavy equipment operator and landscape construction foreman who planted giant specimen trees for a living. He was in high demand because of his unique skills. One customer in particular had a special "we only want Gary for our jobs" request: Jerry Bussell, owner of the renowned Squeeze In Restaurant, famous for the best omelettes on the planet.

Every time Gary did plantings for the restaurant owner, Bussell would request Gary and give him a family gift card at the restaurant as a tip. Misty and Gary fell in love with the Squeeze In — head over heels in love!

Misty had never met Jerry Bussell, but because she loved the restaurant, she revered Jerry too.

Both Gary and Misty started to dream about one day owning The Squeeze In themselves. Many nights, the couple talked about how they could acquire the restaurant and what they would do to run their favorite eatery.

For 15 years they dreamed and fantasized.

By then, Misty had moved up to become a partner in an advertising agency in Reno, Nevada.

One evening, she and her business partner attended a business dinner honoring TV celebrity, Larry King. At the dinner, her partner led Misty and her husband Gary over to a colleague of his, the Governor's Director of Homeland Security. Gary began enthusiastically greeting the director, who coincidentally happened to be none other than Jerry Bussell, Gary's loyal customer and owner of The Squeeze In restaurant.

Misty, after finally meeting Jerry, immediately told him how much they loved eating at the restaurant and asked how it was going there.

Within two weeks, this introduction led to Misty and her PR firm pitching Jerry Bussell a public information campaign for Homeland Security.

After the pitch, Misty again asked Jerry how the Squeeze In was going.

Jerry became very quiet.

Then, he said, "I've been running this business for 26 years and it's going very well. But, I've been thinking of selling it. I'm not going to put it on the market or anything, but I'm thinking about it."

The rest of the meeting was a blur to Misty. She could not focus on the public information campaign. All she could think about was the Squeeze In.

The next morning, Misty waited impatiently as the minutes ticked slowly until 7 AM when she could call Jerry on his cell phone. She asked if he was serious about wanting to sell The Squeeze In.

Jerry said, "Yes, my God, you and Gary would be a perfect fit for this...."

Within a few months, the deal was done, and the transition was made.

Since this new professional door opened for Gary and Misty in 2003, they've grown the Squeeze In from one location with 49 chairs to four locations with almost 400 chairs and are now serving just over a quarter of a million guests annually.

In 2010, word got to Food Network star Bobby Flay and the Youngs were featured on Throwdown with Bobby Flay.

Connecting at the right places with the right people consistently led to Misty's successful career steps.

Misty attributes her connecting success to two key factors:

"Trust your intuition; you can feel when two people's energies are blending."

"Be relentlessly generous. Stinginess breeds stinginess, and the converse is true too: Generosity breeds generosity."

Now that we've explored where you find your ideal Grow Zone connections, it's time to learn how to connect and build rapport with your ideal connections and have them welcome you into their networks.

CHAPTER 4

How To Build Rapport With Ideal Connections And Get Accepted Into The Right Networks

We cannot build our own future without
helping others to build theirs.
—Bill Clinton

Now that you've identified some of the right networking venues for you and your business, the task of getting known, connected, and gaining trust and credibility with new colleagues remains before you. How do you get connected with the right people within these right networks?

Starting out, people don't really know you from Adam. The good news is you have so many tools available to you today to get a big jump on this process.

At the risk of sounding like a nag, I'm going to mention the "R" word again: Research.

Know Thy Network: Leverage The Internet

Once you've chosen one or two key networking niches or arenas to get connected with, you need to let your fingers do the typing and research leaders and members.

Here are several ways you can get a good handle on the people you'll be meeting in these groups and at events you'll be attending.

- ▸ **Identify the heads of committees or leaders** in these groups. Google search them and check out all of their social media pages: LinkedIn, Facebook, Twitter, or other social media pages where they might have posted a profile. Reading about their work history, their accomplishments, where they went to school, and their contacts will help you gain a better feel for areas of common interest, people you know in common (which can speed up your credibility), and give you some relevant facts for opening a strong dialogue with them.

- ▸ **Check out the events calendars** so you learn about the topics and issues addressed by these groups, see who these groups choose as speakers, and get a sense of what these groups are up to in the business community.

- ▸ **Read the association or group's blogs, forums, and list serve message boards.** Here you will learn who the communicators and voices of the groups are and what issues and topics are of interest to this community.

Reach Out And Ask

One of the the best ways to initiate a relationship with a new group is to contact one of the leaders and ask questions about the community. Learning about the membership construct and the goals and direction of the organization gives you a giant leg up on whether this is a good group for you. Simultaneously, you are demonstrating serious interest in their group. If it's a good fit, getting involved in the leadership of the group could be a great direction. Leaders of groups are generally interested in new members who are not only interested in what the group can do for them but what they can do for the group. This is really a win-win situation. Membership-driven networking groups are also focused on growing the ranks of paying members. Any time you can help a group in either of these two objectives, your value and level of respect will escalate.

In most cases, if you are exploring an organization that requires a membership fee, they will allow you to attend one or two meetings or events to experience the group. The questions you want to ask current members are the following to help you evaluate whether this is the right venue for you:

- ▶ What is the overall purpose of the group?
- ▶ How have you benefitted from this group? How long have you been involved?
- ▶ How much time you devoted to the group (this tells you how committed this person is, how much he/she has contributed to the group)
- ▶ What positive benefits/results have you experienced through membership or participation?
- ▶ What has been a disappointment with this organization?
- ▶ What kinds of people do you like to build your network with? (What roles, caliber of people does this person interact with and have in his/her network? What does he/she find is the general make-up of the networks of other members?)

It is important to speak to past members of a group before you join. They can tell you the pros and cons from a different context. You will also want to know what the escape clause is if you are dissatisfied with the group once you join.

There are 3 primary pitfalls people fall into when becoming involved in a for-fee networking group:

1. Not choosing the right group with the right people for your business.
2. Unrealistic expectations — expecting results to happen too quickly.
3. Not contributing to the group or being proactive in meeting with others in the group outside of the scheduled meetings.

I have already discussed how to avoid Pitfall #1. You must research the members of the group, who are in their networks, and what their networking style is. If they are all about themselves and what they are going to get, that tells you a lot of what you will experience once you are a member.

Pitfall #2 is simple but not easy to overcome. I recommend you write down a few "reasonable" objectives from this group experience, and then some "stretch" objectives. Discuss these with the group leader. Check in with him/her to see if your expectations are in alignment with what others have accomplished, and what the group generates.

Pitfall #3 is the most important. Become a producer of connections and opportunities and your visibility, credibility, and opportunities will expand exponentially. Proactive leaders are inspiring and prompt people to spread the good word about you, and are magnetic to the other members. Being proactive, enthusiastic, and energetic by introducing people to one another, inviting people, and generally thinking of how you can help the members of the group, even if you can't provide referrals, will build your personal brand and attract people toward you. This reduces the amount of energy you need to expend "pitching" yourself to others. It's the attract vs. push approach.

My colleague and friend Mark Fishman, a partner in a Los Angeles actuary firm, found out how costly these pitfalls can be:

CASE STUDY

"You join a networking group. You're disappointed because you haven't generated business from this networking group (which frankly costs serious money and takes serious time).

If I had spent more time focusing on finding those particular professionals in the professional network group I joined, considering who I wanted to meet, and made more of a conscious effort to contact them directly in order to get to know them personally, then I would have saved a great deal of time instead of just waiting for the professional network group leaders to put us together. Letting the network group match professionals through their standard process of random troika lunches or breakfasts can take valuable time away from a productive workday. Yes, referrals can come from obscure places and unexpected people, but it's much more efficient to pinpoint the proper target audience and find the time to specifically meet with them. This speeds up the process of starting a business relationship that leads to faster referrals for both professionals."

"It has taken me approximately 2½ years of general meetings, random lunches and breakfasts to get to the right referral professionals, which could have been initiated 2 years sooner had I taken the time to find them within the network myself and make the initial effort to contact them and meet with them. This would have made all the difference in the world in generating referral business faster."

Mark is a very smart guy, so it's not about having the smarts to do the right thing.

The real culprit is lack of training or knowledge about how to strategically build a network. That's why it's so easy to fall into networking pitfalls.

Ultimately, you do want to be connecting with people who have the right mindset and energy level to be out there introducing and connecting in a way similar to you.

Network Like A Fox On Two Important Levels

Naturally, the ultimate objective of networking is to get clients or opportunities and expand your visibility in the marketplace. But in order to do this, you will need to build a network on two levels:

The Introducer/Referrer Level

Your ideal referrer or introducer connections understand you, your talents, your business, and your personal brand (more on personal branding in Chapter 14) and also has relationships with decision makers in your ideal niche market.

These are great relationships to build because when you are introduced through these people, you are vouched for and vetted.

The downside is a referral or introducer can make the warm intro to a prospective client or decision maker but has no direct knowledge of or control over whether that contact will reach out to you or take action on the referral.

The End User /Decision Maker Level

The End User/ Decision Maker is the most direct connection to be made. It's the ultimate goal in the entire networking strategic plan.

So meeting decision maker contacts in your ideal niche market are prime connections.

The downside to connecting with decision makers is you have to cultivate each relationship from scratch.

Your networking strategy should be built on action steps on both of these levels: with referral level contacts and end user/decision makers.

As you choose your networking groups and venues, you will now also be thinking: does this group connect me with referrers or decision makers or both?

Get Involved, Lead The Way

When you are new to a group, it is easy to get lost in the crowd. The fastest and most effective way to get connected and accepted into a new network is to work on a committee. Every group needs its members to volunteer in some way. Taking on leadership or a project on a committee is an invaluable approach to enhance acceptance into a group.

By volunteering for a project you are automatically working with others in the group. This will allow them to get to know you and your work style quickly. Volunteering for a project earns people's appreciation and ultimately their trust as they see you producing results for the group. Everybody is glad that the people who take on assignments are willing to do this. They are grateful and see these people in a positive light.

That being said, it's important to play well in the sandbox so that you are seen as a team player and not as a control-monger or a glory-hound. Contributing your time, new ideas, and working toward the accomplishment of the group's goals is a win-win for you and your community.

Another way of getting connected quickly is to set up brief but focused one-on-one meetings with key members.

In the beginning, one-on-one's can be "getting to know you" in nature, exploratory and relationship-building efforts. As time progresses, you can accelerate the relationship by introducing, inviting, connecting with this person on various professional online networks, and initiating other gestures that show interest and effort.

Ideally, we want to get to know people, and find out how credible and dependable they are. If we are to ultimately refer them and they to refer us, we have to be certain that they will not damage our reputation and integrity. But this is an effort that takes time and a number of subsequent touch points. Remember, the research has shown that it takes seven different touch points for a relationship to develop a level of trust between two people. Most people stop making an effort after touch-point one or two. You must stay persistent and consistent to form the right relationships.

I want to share with you Dawn Levine's story, the story of a lawyer who took on getting involved in the leadership of a networking group and took her network from scratch to sensational:

CASE STUDY
Dawn Levine
Trust & Estates Lawyer
How The New Gal In Town Built Her Top Notch Network & Practice Fast — From Scratch

Dawn Levine was the new gal in town in Cobbs County, Georgia.

Although she had been a successful estate planning attorney before she moved, she was now an unknown and without a network, and needing to build her practice quickly.

Her idea was to take her limited $1000 marketing budget and spend it on advertising in order to get known and drum up business.

Fortunately, Dawn's good friend Alice had experience in advertising and saved the day — and Dawn's $1,000.

Alice told Dawn to go down a different road —she told Dawn to go to lunch.

She said, "Spend your shoestring budget on taking people to lunch."

Dawn loved this idea. The investment was small and she could enjoy the dollars spent at the same time. "Lunch marketing it is, " she decided.

Yet, In the very next moment, Dawn realized that she needed to know people to ask to lunch.

Being the new gal in town also meant having to figure things out for her business on her own. She did a little brainstorming on where she might meet people who could refer business to her, and immediately looked up the local bar association.

As luck would have it, The Cobbs County Bar Association is a very active one. Dawn studied the numerous lunchtime gatherings and decided to start with the solo/small firm section, assuming that many of the attendees would do something other than probate and estate planning.

"It sounded like the right place to start building a network of people who might refer work to me," observes Dawn.

"Conversely, it also occurred to me that it was just as important for me to build a network of people whom I could send cases back to."

"After all, I had no intention of representing car accident victims or divorcing couples or a whole host of other things I might encounter. At the very least, I thought it would be a place I could glean tips about running a solo firm since I had never done that before."

The Solo/Small Firm Section sounded ideal. Upon arrival I wasn't sure I was in the right place. It was meeting time and there were only 3 people in the room! This turned out to be fantastic luck for me. It was election day for the Section. One of the people present was the president who had recently been elected. That left just me and two other members, and they needed a Secretary and a Treasurer. One of the attendees did not want to hold office. By default, I could become an officer just by showing up. Obviously, the section was in trouble as evidenced by the poor turnout. Did I want to do this? I decided I had nothing to lose and at least it was something new to put on my resume. I decided that I would accept the office of Secretary. There was really no pressure since at the moment I only had to serve four people. After the meeting, I went straight across the street and joined the Cobb Bar Association.

During my year as Secretary, the president and I worked together to prevent the section from dying. With a client base of zero, I had plenty of time to work on trying to get speakers for the section, publicizing events and getting people interested in the section again. It was great fun to work on making it grow. As the section grew, my visibility in the county and with other professionals grew, and so did my client base. It almost seemed to grow by itself.

By the end of the year, we had increased attendance by 1000%. Working so hard on revitalizing the section paid off in several ways. At the end of the year the president encouraged me to throw my hat in the ring for president. I did and the members elected me as president of the section. Another something new to put on my resume. The real surprise was when the president, Jack Lyle, asked me to become a named partner in his firm. Over the year we worked on the section, I had learned of his great reputation for his ethics and legal ability. To say I was deeply honored is an understatement.

I could not sleep for three days while I thought about it and discussed it with my family. Of course, I accepted. Now we are Lyle & Levine, LLC, growing by leaps and bounds.

If all of that wasn't enough of a windfall for just showing up that day, I have had all sorts of other opportunities come my way. Being an officer in the section gave me many opportunities to get noticed and get business. I was able to meet established colleagues in the area on a more even footing than if I was just another attorney in the community.

It can be difficult to approach a stranger to say 'please send me business'. It sounds desperate, it feels desperate. However, it is easy to approach people if you are telling them about something that is of interest to them. 'Hey did you hear about our CLE on marketing this month.' Being an officer gave me an opportunity to approach everyone who attended our section meetings to make them feel welcome. It was my business to find out what their practice area is, what kind of business they are looking for, and learn more about them. It gave me opportunities to help connect them to other members in the section for mutually beneficial referrals. It was helpful to them, made me a valuable resource, and was great fun. It also gave me an inroad to talk to members and officers of other sections.

I got all the same opportunities with the members of the Elder Law Section, the Business Law Section, etc. It also gave me a chance to meet the Cobb Bar's Board of Trustees, the leaders of our local legal community. They run the legal show, so to speak, and I had things to tell them that were of interest to them. They noticed the hard work Jack and I did to bring the section back from the brink. This led to an opportunity to serve and meet the entire Cobb Bar as Trustee-at-large and then Secretary.

I have gone from a client base of zero to a partner in a law firm and multiple leadership roles, all from working on a leadership committee and being willing to help.

My biggest pearl of networking wisdom to the readers of this book is to focus on others. If you are only thinking of yourself, talking about yourself and focused on what you can get for yourself, it will be obvious. If you find yourself on the receiving end of this, excuse yourself quickly but, politely.

Really listen to the person in front of you. What can you do for them? Can you send them business? Can you connect their daughter to someone looking for summer help? Is there an article on your desk that they might be helpful to them? I have helped people find back surgeons, custom jewelry designers, jobs, pet sitters, articles on nutrition, other attorneys, of course, and whatever else they are looking for. I always try to send an email if I see someone I know mentioned in the paper. Introducing people who can benefit each other is another example. If I introduce my favorite accountant to my dry cleaner, I get no direct benefit. However, if they are a good fit, I have helped them both and they think I am a valuable resource. The side benefit is it is fun.

Blogging, Guest Blogging, And Article Writing To Build Trust
Blogging can take a considerable amount of time and effort, and it may not be for you if you are not a comfortable writer. That doesn't necessarily leave you out in the blogosphere cold. You can also gain a considerable amount of traction and give credibility to other member's blogs by commenting on their posts. That may even work better for you and for your new contacts. Everyone who blogs wants more readers and interactivity on their blog. Your comments will be

immensely appreciated. It's a quick way to connect with the blogger and the blogger's community.

As you meet new people at networking events, ask them if they have a blog. A quick way to build rapport with a new colleague is to read their blog, let them know you've checked out their work and comment. In today's heavily competitive blogging community, nothing will warm up a new relationship faster than letting someone know you read their blog and took the time to comment. You will want to be smart about this. Commenting on blogs that are in alignment with your target market will encourage some readers to also follow you in your own blog after they read what you have to say.

A former law firm client of mine had launched a blog. I noticed that a local TV show featured their blog. I immediately sent a note to the head of the firm's marketing department congratulating her on this visibility. She didn't even know the blog had been featured and thanked me profusely. Do you think she was pleased that I was thinking of her and her firm? Soon after, she referred me to a colleague of hers.

Your group may very well have a newsletter that they send to members. Offering to contribute content or an article is an ideal way to get connected to this community. Think of value-added topics that you can write on or research. Newsletter editors are always eager for content because that's their main objective — They are hungry for great content. They are usually doing this on a volunteer basis in addition to their main job, so helping them fulfill this objective is a great relief.

Taking this idea to the next level, not only can you provide content, but you can also help the newsletter editors get articles and content from your contacts. The more you assist members of your networking community, especially in ways that gains them visibility and free PR, the more valuable and visible you become. This will certainly speed up the process of your getting accepted and known in a favorable way.

Become A Cheerleader: Invite Guests

Once you are familiar with your networking group and you have a sense of the energy, the people, the productivity, and the networks of the people in the organization, you will have a feeling of confidence about whether you want to invite your other trusted contacts into this community.

Some groups are happy to stay at their current size. Others are looking to build membership. If you are feeling confident that this group is one you plan to stay in and support, a key way to increase your stature within is to invite others to become members.

Most groups have guest days or meeting segments where prospective members can attend and get a "taste" of the organization. Your guest choices are really important. Make sure to bring people who would be a good fit, not just anybody so you fulfill the expectation of bringing guests.

While these organizations do want quality members, they also often feel driven to fulfill the numbers. Maybe they need membership dues; maybe they need to fulfill certain areas of expertise in the group. Regardless, the leaders often desire quality members but get sidetracked by the need for revenue and bodies attending.

Your challenge is to bring quality people to the table. Think about this as you invite. You will gain tremendous appreciation and credibility by bringing the right people to the right groups. Your guests will appreciate your thinking of them to offer opportunity, and your organization will appreciate your careful evaluation of the right folks for them.

You've Gotta Have A Gimmick (Or How Compelling Is My Elevator Speech?)

So much has been written and said about 'The Elevator Speech' that it almost seems redundant to discuss it in this book. What I'd like to do is give you some advanced strategic ways you can craft and leverage this ubiquitous networking tool.

You absolutely should have an elevator speech, but not only for the traditionally accepted reasons.

One of the biggest benefits of working on your elevator speech, or your 30-second "commercial" about what you do and why it's distinctive/valuable, is not only so that others will know about you and your business, but **because you need to get clear on this yourself.**

How will others be able to refer business to you if they're not sure exactly what you do, why it's beneficial, who it's relevant for, or sold on your value?

Ninety percent of the people I speak to know the first part: what they do. Only about ten percent of the people I speak to know why they are distinctive compared to all the other people in their field, or why this is relevant or particularly valuable for the people they are interested in working with or marketing to. They don't have clarity about the specifics of their ideal client, their unique value proposition, and are generally spouting trite statements about high quality and integrity as if those are unique characteristics. Worse, people are often including lower pricing in their elevator speech.

Folks, quality and integrity are the price of entry!

I was at a meeting the other day and a woman gave a testimonial to another member in the room and emphasized her low prices! This member had touted lower fees and guess what? Her praiser regurgitated it to everyone in the room. What does this woman stand for in the minds of everyone? You got it: low fees.

This is such a dangerous strategy because it invites competitors to undercut you in price, leaving you with little or no competitive advantage.

When working on your differentiation statement focus strongly on what's different about you that **means something to me. What's in it for me** to work with you?

That's what people are listening for: What's In It For Me?

That's why I think one of the most important benefits of working on your elevator speech is so that you are clear, and I mean **crystal**

clear, about why you are the go-to person, the go-to firm, why people should hire you or buy from you particularly.

Most advice about elevator speeches still makes the process too long, too complicated, too much about you, not compelling enough for the listener, and definitely not interesting.

It's a formidable task to entice people to hear more about you in one or two short sentences, and to deliver it in such a way that is natural and engaging. As short and powerful as it must be (15–30 seconds) it takes a considerable amount of effort to craft and hone this essential tool. Few of us spend much effort on it, and just expect that "winging it" will attract referrals and clients.

Furthermore, few spend much time on getting clear about the characteristics and demographics of ideal clients. No wonder you're not meeting as many of them as you'd like!

In 1962, Rosalind Russell and Natalie Wood starred in the block-buster movie, *Gypsy*, the story of a vaudevillian mother who wanted her daughter to be a star on stage. Ultimately, her daughter Rose did became a star, as one of the most famous strippers of all time. Rose got some powerful mentoring from veteran strippers. In the lyrics of the song "You Gotta Get A Gimmick" we gain some cut-to-the-chase marketing wisdom:

"You gotta have a gimmick if you want to get ahead."

Do gimmicks sound too contrived to you? Understandably so, but the essential point here is you have to figure out: what's your thing? Why you? over all the hundreds or thousands of others who do what you do.

You need to know exactly who you want to work with and who you want to attract.

You need to know why you are the right person for them to work with over all the others.

You need to be crystal clear about why these folks will want and need to work with you — now or in the future — (what are their pain points?) and why your solutions are perfect for them.

You need to be able to articulate all of this with confidence.

AND

You need to be able to have people want to listen to you in the first place.

Having a "unique value proposition" or the business version of a "gimmick" is an essential ingredient in your networking strategy.

Because you may select more than one market or niche segment for your business, it's best to create an elevator speech tailored to each market. The more your value proposition is designed specifically for a particular niche market, the more appealing it will be. Don't shy away from creating more than one elevator speech for different audiences if you want to attract more than one population.

I always think examples are really good ways to "get" the picture of how you might craft your message.

And giving people "visuals" of who you are and what you might do for them is a key way for people to remember you and want to learn more about you.

Here are a few of my favorites elevator speeches:

It can't be easy for an accountant to create an interesting or memorable elevator speech. Yet, one resourceful accountant spent real effort in crafting one of the shortest and yet most compelling elevator speeches I've heard:

I'm not the best accountant in the world, but I'm a great businessman and know how to make businesses profitable. If you're looking to make your business more profitable, we should talk.

Let's analyze this for a moment. There are many strategically effective and powerful elements in this elevator speech:

- ▸ Short. Two brief sentences.
- ▸ He diminished the official title of "accountant" because he knew that this was more of a commodity role. Also he humbled himself.
- ▸ He talked about his major value proposition (in a short, succinct statement): He knows how to make businesses profitable. Who doesn't want their business to be profitable or more profitable?
- ▸ He invited the other person to speak with him if there was interest in this sort of an invitation. But he did it with a direct, non-pushy statement.
- ▸ Because he downplayed himself and then built up his key area of value, it is a memorable approach. Few people have the courage to own up not being great at something.

It took a lot of work to boil all the possibilities into such a short, succinct, powerful, memorable statement that clearly tells other people what's in it for them to work with him.

Here's one of mine:

I advise lawyers, accountants and service entrepreneurs how to eliminate their fear about selling and get higher paying clients. I show them how to become the go-to firm in profitable niche markets.

Short, to the point, with specific benefit statements. Memorable phrases are: Higher paying clients. Who doesn't want that? Becoming the go-to firm. In a competitive market, professionals want a way to stand out from their competition. I was also specific in the niche clients I specialize in.

Being clear with your ideal "sweet spot" connections will be very helpful in opening the door to your new connections. Your attentive listening to their elevator speech will go a long way to building deeper bonds with them.

In The End, You Get What You Give

Getting connected in your ideal communities is one part consistent activity and three parts patience. You must stay committed even if people take some time before embracing you into their fold. In the beginning, you'll probably find it necessary to give a lot to the community until you are trusted, included, and remembered by your community. It's not personal, it's just human nature.

The biggest error people make when starting to network is what I call the flash approach: They go out there and start networking everywhere in a big burst of energy. Then, because they don't have a plan or they have expectations about fast results, they get disillusioned and stop following up or maintain consistency.

Consistency is one of the most important elements you need to infuse into your "network like a fox" plan.

In fact, let's hear from a savvy Director of Sales and what he learned the hard way about networking:

CASE STUDY

Maurice Diab

Director of Sales

DocuSource

A Sales Leader Learns The Secret To Targeted Networking: Consistency Is Key

Maurice Diab has been a pro in business to business sales for over a decade. As the director of sales for a mid-sized document management company, his accountability is not only for his own success but mentoring and guiding his team of 12 to success in their sales results as well.

Any great sales leader knows from personal experience how steep the learning curve going from sales person to sales leader can be.

So when Maurice advanced from sales person to sales director, he knew that he'd have to set the right example and walk the talk for building the right customer relationships if he wanted his sales team to be successful too.

At Maurice's company, Docusource, a growing mid-sized document management company, he and his sales group are working within a highly competitive industry.

Therefore the lead generation process can be very challenging. Maurice sees how important it is to designate their market differentiators.

What he's found? It's rarely price; it often isn't even the product that wins the customer.

It's the service approach and level.

Many sales candidates believe that success in an interview will be based on smart answers about selling.

Maurice Diab looks at sales success and sales potential with a different eye.

When determining how strong a potential sales rep will be he looks at several factors:

- the size and quality of their network,
- how many LinkedIn contacts they have and
- how they answer this question at networking events, "So what do you do?"

Maurice feels networking skills are so critical to sales talent hiring decisions, he highlights these skills as prerequisite to bringing someone on his team and has a series of networking-related interview questions.

What's he really looking for?

Getting a sense of how his candidates approach and succeed at building the right network.

When asked what makes the difference between a good networker and a great networker, Maurice says:

Good networkers are good at tapping the usual people networks — people they work with, those they interact with personally, in their neighborhoods, etc.

"The great networkers can get to **the right people**, can gain their trust, connect with other influential connectors, as Malcolm Gladwell points out in his best-selling book, The Tipping Point," he says.

"These connectors then will praise your work to others and open many doors and expand your ideal network."

Maurice looks back and sees that his networking skills needed a lot of work in the beginning, and had to be honed.

His biggest regret? He was inconsistent in his networking approach.

He'd be solid at it for several months, then slack off. He says he may have missed out on building trust with a number of good people that way.

Now he knows that consistent participation on committees with the right organizations or having a leadership role helps create and build that trust outside of that organization.

The other mistake he's worked to correct and teaches to his team? "Where's the order?" thinking.

He overcame that mindset when he connected two networking colleagues, helped them create an opportunity, and ultimately built trust for future business with each of them.

This fostered his current "How Can I Help Them?" approach to networking.

The mistakes he sees his team making are often the ones he made when he began. One of the most glaring ones is networking at the wrong level — i.e. networking down vs. networking up with decision makers.

"It really is easier and smarter to network at a higher level, go down a level or two to get the information you need, then circle back with that top level to close the loop and land the business." He encourages his sales team to network with the right decision makers and influencers as often as possible.

However, Maurice Diab still continues to remind his team about the need for consistency and targeted networking to keep the business pipeline flowing with the right relationships.

CHAPTER 5

Overcoming I'm Too… (Young, Old, Busy, Afraid) To Network With The Right People

I HAVE WORKED WITH and spoken with people of all ages, genders, professions, races and ethnic groups.

One of the biggest areas that business people struggle with is self-confidence.

Issues with self-confidence usually shows up in two ways:

Avoidance due to lack of self-confidence, or arrogance.

Both are signals of uncertainty about oneself.

I have watched many people hug the walls or clam up in shyness and I have observed outwardly "self-confident" people who cover up their lack of confidence with swagger and self-importance. I'll speak more about this in the section on Authenticity.

If you have ever been nervous or uncomfortable about walking into a room of high powered strangers, join the crowd. Maybe you've even heard yourself voicing one or more of these explanations (i.e. excuses) for why you aren't attending the very groups or events where you'd likely meet your Grow Zone audience:

"I'm too young"

"I'm too old"

"I'm not at the level of that group"

"I don't have the time"

"My client work takes precedence"

"My wife/husband expects me home"

"I don't really need to network for my job"

I've heard just about every excuse in the book about why networking takes a back seat to everything else in businesses.

Every excuse you make gives you a big pay-off and not a good one. When I say this to people, they scratch their heads in bewilderment.

It's not so complicated.

Your excuses and reasons may seem valid, but they are all a smokescreen to feel justified in staying stuck and not achieving what you say you want. Trust me when I tell you that people do exactly and only what they truly want to do. How do I know this? Take a look at what they are actually doing. That's what they want to be doing.

People say they want a happy marriage; then they avoid communication or go out and have affairs.

They say they want a better job. What do they do? Complain a lot, but do very little work on the resume or networking with the right people to make new things happen.

They say they want new business, and they go to a networking event sporadically and forget to do the important follow-up. Then they wonder why they don't get new business from networking.

They say they want to be successful but let fear, issues with self-confidence stop them from doing what would actually give them ideal connections, new business and ultimately more self confidence:

Are you stopping yourself from doing the very things that will eliminate the problem?

Self-Confidence Is The Problem

My client Allen, in his mid-fifties, is painfully shy. He had been trained to be a hard worker, follow instructions, study diligently and be very smart at what he does in order to "succeed" in life. For him, making a change in approach was like turning the Titanic around. However, it was eating away at him that younger, less knowledgeable people were being promoted and bringing in business. He just didn't know what to do about it.

I'd love to tell you that once we started working together Allen had a miraculous transformation. Not so. Week after week he'd come to our meetings not having done much or any of the things I had assigned. I eventually said that there wasn't much point to going forward; he was going to have to make a decision for himself whether he'd break through this inertia.

But wait!

One of the things we had talked about was how he was relatively "unknown" in his own firm. I gave him a last assignment: get a mentor in the firm who was one of the influencers, someone on the executive committee, someone who had clout in the company. A "right" person. Requesting a mentor was an easy way to access a key person and "get known."

In just a few months, Allen was promoted to partner. He came to my office one day to thank me.

I asked him why he was thanking me. He said, "I took your advice and got Joe as my mentor. After working together for six months, he got to see what I had to offer the firm and more about who I was. I believe he pushed the executive committee to promote me."

The good news doesn't end there.

Another few months went by. Again, Allen came to my office and asked, "Did you hear the news?" I said,

"What news?" He said, "I just brought in a $130K client." I said, "Take a seat and tell me the whole story."

Apparently, one of Allen's partners had passed some work to him. The client happened to be a hugely successful celebrity with several business entities. Allen was well liked by this client's business manager because he was attentive, accurate, and brought new ideas to the table. The relationship expanded. One day, Allen noticed that this client could benefit by an additional service the firm provided and mentioned his thoughts to the business manager. That turned into a presentation for additional services and ultimately a 40% growth in that account.

This success gave Allen a big boost in confidence. It prompted him to call an attorney friend with whom he hadn't spoken in a while just to say hi and see what was new with him. That conversation led to the attorney referring a lead to Allen. That lead turned into a request to pitch new business. Allen brought his mentor Joe to the pitch, and they landed a new client generating about $130K to the firm.

Now, Allen was bitten by the rainmaking bug.

One little step toward confidence led to another step, and eventually his self-confidence was where it always could have and should have been. I believe that the confidence in Allen's voice when he called the referring attorney contributed to that lawyer offering him the business opportunity. After all, why had he never offered anything to Allen before?

We train people how to regard us. The next thing I am about to tell you is key:

> Self-confidence is not something we acquire.
> It is something that is already present in each of us.
> All we have to do is access it.

For those who feel uncomfortable about meeting and speaking to influencers and decision makers because they are too young, I suggest you go back to Chapter 1 and read the story about Brian, our young professional who networked his way to partner in a fraction of the time of fellow professionals.

I hear this concern from young professionals all the time: "I just don't feel comfortable talking to older, more experienced (and successful) people because I don't have anything to offer them or have anything in common with them. I don't know what to say to them."

I recall attending a wonderful networking event a few years ago at a fantastic location with a stunning view of New York City. The venue was spectacular, food and drink were abundant, and the 100 attendees included a wonderful mix of executives and professionals from high quality companies and firms. The speaker was the CEO of a major bank. In this room, the decision makers of major companies were present.

I looked around the room and noticed the following: There were groups of 3 and 4 people around the room, chatting and drinking. There were groups of mature business people, and then scattered around the room, the younger people were also chatting — with each other. They were not mingling with the more senior decision makers. I thought to myself — what a missed opportunity!

I made my way over to a few of these groups of young professionals and after listening and chatting lightly with them, I asked, "Is there a reason you are mingling with other young professionals and not chatting with the more senior level folks here tonight?" They were embarrassed and said they felt uncomfortable breaking into conversation with more experienced and senior executives.

How do you develop a network of influencers and decision makers when you are significantly less experienced or not at the same level as them? How does one create relationships and engage in meaningful dialogue when one has a high discomfort level about this?

Nike has the most effective answer: "Just do it."

I'd like to introduce you to Richard Strauss, of Strauss Radio. Let's look at how he overcame his lack of self-confidence and transformed not only his career but that of a pretty influential person as well:

CASE STUDY
Richard Strauss
How The 3-Second Rule Helped
A Shy Guy Help Bill Clinton

In December 2007, PR Week named Richard Strauss to their inaugural "40 Under 40", recognizing and profiling 40 PR pros, nominated by industry peers, who have achieved tremendous feats prior to turning 40.

But how he got here had a lot to do with whom he met along the way.

Richard learned very early in his career that meeting the right people made a huge difference in one's life. Starting as a reporter for a small newspaper during college at UCLA, he also worked at the college radio station. He interviewed some heavy hitters such as Dusty Baker, coach of the LA Dodgers, and Dr. Ruth Westheimer. He even interviewed Larry King during the era when Larry was a radio host. Although Richard wasn't with a major publication, he was able to get coverage of Magic Johnson's announcement of his retirement from basketball because a fellow-reporter friend of his helped to sneak him into the press conference.

Using connections at his local Congressman's office, Richard applied for media credentials as a reporter for the 1988 Democratic Convention in Atlanta. He was rejected because he applied too late. Undaunted and determined to still work in politics, four years later, his father, always a proponent of strong connections, suggested that Richard check out Bill Clinton, a Democratic political candidate gaining a lot of interest. Richard dialed 411 in Little Rock, Arkansas and "met" Steven Cohen, Executive Assistant to campaign press secretary Dee Dee Myers. Cohen greenlit Richard's interview in New Hampshire because in the conversation Richard mentioned he had radio experience.

He flew to New Hampshire on a $99 certificate he had saved. On the very day of his interview, he found himself shoved into a receiving line where he met none other than the promising candidate himself. He was offered a volunteer position and decided to leave college to work as a volunteer on the campaign.

Working side by side with some of the most brilliant and innovative political strategists and influencers gave him not only the insight and experience of working in the communications and political arena, but relationships that impacted his life forever. He was mentored by some of the outstanding experts of the Clinton era: David Wilhelm, Jeffrey Eller, George Stephanopoulos, Mickey Kantor, and then later, David Gergan. Richard was later invited to be part of the White House staff where he served three years as the first-ever White House Radio Director. In this capacity, Strauss was responsible for coordinating and producing President Clinton's weekly Saturday morning radio address. On the day of the first Clinton address, he walked into the Oval for the first time. There, sitting behind the famous desk, was Bill. Seeing Richard's awe at entering the history-filled room, he said to Richard: "You know, Richard, I was a little overwhelmed the first time I came into this room too! I think you're going to be okay."

Richard lived the West Wing life for a while, and credits his relationships with all of the Clinton Administration icons as helping him build a very successful career. He saw being part of this influential community, and one that was willing to mentor and introduce him to others who could help him advance, as being a key element in who he has become today.

As a very young man, Richard had to overcome great shyness to take the steps necessary to converse and interact with experienced and powerful people. He adopted the Nike philosophy: "Just Do It" but advises people use a method which he calls, "The 3-Second Rule": When you're nervous about approaching someone, you give yourself 3 seconds and then you just GO!

I can certainly relate to the fear and discomfort felt by most people about meeting and talking to big cheeses. Early on, I too struggled with lack of confidence when it came to meeting higher level decision makers and influencers.

How should I initiate a conversation? How could I find out who they are without sounding foolish.

To make matters more difficult, very often, high level movers and shakers aren't wearing a name tag with their title or job description.

So how do you meet and meld with someone who is a bigger cheese?

After a lot of trial and error, I developed a sort of script to help me break the ice with big cheeses.

This opener seems to easily help me quickly learn who I'm speaking with in a way that doesn't make me feel inferior or make the person I'm speaking with uncomfortable.

My little script sounds something like:

"It's a pleasure to meet you Adam; would you mind telling me your role in your company (or organization)?"

If their name tag mentions their company, that's helpful and I will name the company when I ask the question.

If not, I will ask the person to tell me about their role and their company.

In this way I've met the CEO of major corporations, government officials, and it's resulted in some delightful conversations. Once I know who I'm speaking with I can begin to ask questions that will open up a dialogue.

There is an important secret about self-confidence and networking that I want to share with you, especially as you start to elevate your level of connections in different networking venues.

When I interviewed some pretty high level business owners and executives about networking, to a person, they admitted that they too were nervous entering a room full of strangers and uncomfortable breaking the ice with people they hadn't met before.

In other words, big cheeses are nervous about networking too.

When I learned this, it really leveled the playing field for me. We are all dealing with a natural human discomfort with how to break the ice with new people.

Meet Cindy Rakowitz, PR expert. Cindy's networking talents were hard-earned, even though she started out hobnobbing with lots of higher-ups.

CASE STUDY
Cindy Rakowitz
Public Relations Expert,
Author on Crisis Management
A Playboy Enterprises Exec Networks Her Way
To Entrepreneurial Success

Cindy Rakowitz is a two-time winner. But it wasn't the lottery or luck that earned her these successes. She did it by building one outstanding relationship at a time.

When in her 20's, her willingness to start at the bottom, work hard, and show undying dedication paid off. She was swiftly noticed and rewarded by top management at her first employer, WOR-TV in NYC.

The station's General Manager, Robert Fenimore, recognized her talent and moved her up and into the publicity department within 6 months.

Then a new General Manager came in (changes at the top can be very good for one's career). Peter Leone moved quickly and made Cindy head of the publicity department.

Young, relatively new to this business, and almost unable to believe her good fortune, Cindy now found herself seated at the same table with the honchos — veteran department heads making huge policy decisions.

Peter Leone, the big cheese, had Cindy's back, and fortuitously propelled Cindy into the world of public relations leadership.

Cindy's visibility and credibility escalated, and she began to be recognized by more senior layers in the corporation. This led to her being recruited for the corporate director position. At this level, she was now being mentored by the likes of Steve Ellis, who taught her about crisis management. Firsthand, she was thrown into the midst of a firestorm when RKO was dealing with hostile media, government relations problems, and frightened employees and customers during an international misconduct matter.

This kind of visibility and increased credibility while swimming with the big boys and girls attracted attention from other movers and shakers in the media world, including a turning-point phone call from Playboy Enterprises.

Cindy jumped at the chance to join PEI and be mentored by the likes of division President, Michael Perlis, editorial director, Arthur Kretchmer, as well as CEO Christie Hefner and the iconic founder, Hugh Hefner.

Mike Perlis and Cindy forged a strong business bond through a similar work ethic and values. His supportive mentoring of Cindy helped overcome Christie Hefner's doubts about promoting Cindy. But his influence led to winning Christie's OK to elevate Cindy to Corporate Vice President. This was echoed by Arthur Kretchmer, so Cindy had two superstars endorsing her.

Now, Cindy had a direct line to two of the most powerful media moguls in the industry:

Christie Hefner and Hugh M. Hefner.

Looking back, Cindy attributes her success to being linked with the top echelon of the media world, her devotion to perfection, exceptional work ethic, and outstanding mentors.

But always eager to grow and expand, after a stellar corporate career, Cindy decided to go off on her own and start her own Public Relations venture.

There were some real challenges forcing Cindy to grow in ways she hadn't planned on.

She came out of her corporate background "cocky." Cindy reasoned, "If I had overcome tremendous obstacles before in my early career, then surely I could "kill it" as an entrepreneur, right?"

Wrong.

"It was part of my job description at Playboy Enterprises to mold people into thinking the right way. When I tried to mold people into thinking the right way as an entrepreneur, I failed miserably. "

"There are two important things I learned: Humility and taking more time to evaluate and build relationships with the right people.

"I had to learn completely new ways of operating with people.

"When I was under the corporate umbrella, by association and position, I had immediate clout and credibility. It was easy for me to contact anyone on Christie or Hugh Hefner's list because I was calling on behalf of them.

"If Farrah Fawcett was scheduled to shoot an upcoming pictorial, I would be her first contact while she was meeting with the photography/TV production staff.

"If Hef was having a casual meeting with Brian Grazer in the Mansion library, he'd make an immediate introduction when I walked in the room.

"Access and connection to the most influential was a daily occurrence.

"Which is also what made the transition to going out on my own so difficult.

"I had to learn to make my own contacts and connections when I 'retired from royalty.'

"I may have had a relationship with the 'royal palace' but I chose to leave it."

So being cocky led to a very humbling experience. Cindy's expectations were unrealistic.

"The good news is eventually I learned to find a way to operate in my own palace.

"I began to find the right places to network. I joined an organization called ProVisors in California and met some excellent professionals. I was learning to network differently.

"Today, I have a thriving public relations business that I love, and I have the freedom to work on projects that are challenging and stimulating, such as the book I co-authored that's been inside of me for a long time: *Emergency Public Relations: Crisis Management in a 3.0 World*."

Self-confidence is something everyone grapples with when it comes to meeting the right people.

Another woman who has worked hard to develop her self-confidence and has succeeded is Laura Banks. It's well known that performers are often highly insecure and struggle with self-confidence. Laura is a successful comedienne as well as an entrepreneur. She has leveraged a great networking strategy and shares her tips on how you can build your self-confidence to network up.

CASE STUDY
Laura Banks
Best Selling Author,
Stand Up Comic, Entrepreneur

Creativity and ideas are only the first step in making things happen in business.

You gotta meet the right people to bring those ideas to reality.

As an author (including Breaking The Rules, a USA Today bestseller), actress, stand-up comic, and radio talk show host, traveling in like-minded circles led me to people with whom I resonated and who eventually helped me achieve tremendous success.

However, networking with and meeting the right people isn't only about opening the right doors for business. It also can lead you to finding ideal strategic partners who complement your talents, and allow you to accomplish things you could never do on your own.

When I was working in public relations at a casting office in LA, I met a man who was lecturing on nutrition for one of the performers. That lecturer turned out to be Dr. Alan H. Pressman.

Alan is a nutritional and health expert. He saw my talent for creating original radio programming and he wanted to bring his mission to more people. This complimented my expertise as a talk show host. With my abilities in production and networking, and his on-air work, this led to a highly productive and successful partnership as co-owners of Primary Nutrients. That chance meeting turned into Alan hosting radio infomercials on over 1000 radio stations, and my producing Healthline Radio on WWRL, 1600 AM and WVNJ, New Jersey, and our joint website, www.pressman-health.com which has received over one-million hits.

Another example of how networking brings the right people into partnership, I was at a stand-up comedy show produced by Lifetime TV. There, I met the amazing Janette Barber.

Janette Barber is a fellow stand-up comic as well as a television producer, and writer. She has won six Emmy Awards. Ultimately, Janette became my co-author on two books, one of which became a USA Today bestseller, Breaking The Rules, and our newest book, Embracing Your Big Fat Ass.

I invited Janette to my home for a writer's group meeting, and we saw that we were a perfect match. Again, we complement each other: Janette is the details and follow-through, I am the idea machine.

This theme of meeting the right people through the right performance circles persisted because I also met Peter Miller, my literary manager at a one person show. Standing in the lobby, we started chatting and the rest is history.

The right people, as I would define it, instantly become participants in your life in a big way.

There are two things that I think are essential for finding and connecting with the right people:

The first is intuition (I knew Alan Pressman was going to be in my life the second I heard his voice over the phone).

The second element is confidence. Generating confidence is done when you are true to yourself and your interests. I will always have a project or a reason to be in communication with people whom I admire and with whom I want to interact.

When working on meeting ideal influential people, self-confidence is so important. A tip for people who want to develop greater self-confidence: take an acting class, get on stage. Get in front of people, work through any discomfort about public speaking — all else will follow.

If I could be in any one's circle now, I'd choose Jay Abraham and Carrie Fisher.

Jay is a master marketer. Carrie, is just friggin' funny — she inspires me.

One big mistake I made along the way, i.e. connecting with the wrong people, is confusing money for success. When you interact with people who don't treat you with respect or who don't share your values, it's a success-drain. I will never make that mistake again.

Connecting with the right people has made me financially successful, a published author, and allowed me to reach thousands of people to share my point of view through my books and radio.

Laura is not an introvert by any means. That doesn't mean she hasn't had to be strategic about meeting the right people. Her story demonstrates that.

If you've ever heard Derek Halpern, founder of the enormously successful blog, Social Triggers, on one of his webinars or podcasts, you'd think he was a born performer, speaker, and huge extrovert. In truth, the guy is the proverbial introvert.

In an interview I had with Derek, I asked him how he found the courage and the means to connect with some of the top bloggers and get them to feature him on their sites. He answered my question with this question: Have you ever seen The Hip Hop Preacher's video on YouTube entitled:

How Bad Do You Want It? (I hadn't but immediately checked it out — and I suggest you do too)

Derek obviously wanted it bad enough to ignore his shyness and fear, to think of ways he could be helpful to heavy hitters in the blogging world. He did all of this so they'd talk him up on their sites. Derek reached out to every top dog he could find, didn't let the word "no" stop him, and just kept plugging away, offering to help big bloggers with better ways to feature their work online. As a result they talked Derek up, and he built more and more traffic to his blog in the process. How Bad Do YOU Want It? For a practical approach, read on.

What Is Your BIG WHY?

For those who tell me they lack self-confidence to get out there and meet people, network and get leads and clients, I ask you to ask yourself, "What is your Big Why in life?"

If you are telling yourself and everyone around you about all the things you want to do and have, and you haven't taken those actions that would lead you to getting them, what's missing for you is connecting to the powerful purpose behind achieving those dreams and goals. Without what I call The Big Why you will not do what is necessary or what is uncomfortable. This is how people get stopped.

For some people, The Big Why is success, or recognition, or money, or providing for their families. For others, it is a cause, or making a difference, or having an impact in a particular arena. Whatever drives and moves you can be the motivating force to help you through the disappointments and fearful times when results are taking too long and you have to feel the discomfort of doing things you'd rather not be doing.

What was Michael Jordan's Big Why in continuing to practice after his high school coach refused to put him on the varsity team?

What was Steve Job's Big Why in rejoining Apple after being tossed out years before?

What is your Big Why for producing the results you say you want?

Determination Beats Out Degrees

Another client of mine is an extraordinary example of how a BIG WHY and the desire to produce results overcame his lack of confidence.

Jeff didn't start out with a great network. He wasn't the most handsome guy around. He was on the short side (for men in business this can be experienced as a confidence-deflater). He wasn't the smartest or the most technically astute. And Jeff wasn't comfortable talking to people. But he was determined not to let any of that stop him.

In order to be a successful provider for his family (his BIG WHY) Jeff pushed himself to consistently meet with people. He forced himself and was willing to "be uncomfortable" long enough until his lack of confidence was outweighed by his experience in helping other business people succeed. Once he started to build a track record with other business people, people started flocking to Jeff. He built a successful company with hundreds of employees. Today, Jeff leads his company with "tough love" and a great sense of humor. You'd never guess he was an insecure, shy guy by nature. Now his BIG WHY is to maintain his success and take his company to a new level. But there's an even BIGGER WHY. Jeff gets a great deal of personal satisfaction helping his employees thrive. His mission is to make his company a dependable home so his employees can make a good living. He takes enormous pleasure in giving people solid career opportunities to be as successful as they want to be — IF they do the necessary work.

You Have To Give Confidence To Gain It

I've been doing a lot of talking about self-confidence in a book about networking.

Why?

Because even though I can tell you exactly what to do and how to do it to be a successful networker, if your self-confidence is low, you will not have the mental muscle to take these actions consistently.

That's why building your self-confidence muscle is so important.

And for most people this confidence is in easier reach than you realize.

The ridiculous thing about self-confidence is that everyone could have it, and I am not talking about arrogance here. Arrogance is actually a lack of self-confidence, covered up by bravado.

After my first few years in the coaching business, I really felt as though I had come into my own, and I started thinking about the magnitude of making a difference in people's lives. I knew that this was a valuable, gratifying way of earning a living. Sounds altruistic, right?

Not.

Because, in the next moment, I had this aha! realization: Everything I was doing was self-oriented.

By working with others and helping them be successful, I was gaining confidence. I was feeling good about myself. I was doing something of value for others, so I felt good about me.

Hmmm — so if I gave other's confidence, then I would have it?

This was a completely different way of looking at how to access self-confidence.

How about you? Here are some basics on building self-confidence that could save you thousands of dollars in the therapist's office. (I'm not saying that traditional talk therapy doesn't provide value; rather, these basics can add to what therapy offers and maybe even speed up the process.)

So here's what I've learned about self-confidence:

- ▸ You have to give it to gain it.
- ▸ You have to dig deep inside of yourself to access it; it comes from within, not from without.
- ▸ You have to be interested in others for them to be interested in you.
- ▸ Focusing on being helpful to others always gives you a sense of confidence; focusing on yourself rarely does.
- ▸ You have to ACT AS IF. When you act uncertain or don't believe in yourself, no one else will believe in you. People follow your lead, so ACT AS IF you are already confident and others will naturally gravitate toward your confidence.
- ▸ Generosity and helping others gives you a feeling of power and helps you build your confidence, so find ways of helping others in their business.

You don't have to be the most experienced or most knowledge-able person in the room to warrant self-confidence. These methods do start to turn the tide on self-confidence.

A Word About Being Too Busy

The number one reason (i.e. excuse) people give me for not network-ing consistently is that they are too busy. They have too much work or too many other pressing responsibilities to carve out some time each month to build the right network.

I know this is an excuse because after years of coaching hundreds of people, I have learned one constant: People do EXACTLY what they want to do.

How is it that people are too busy to network but they can play video games or be a couch potato or sit in the company lunchroom BS'ing with the same people day after day for hours? They could have been meeting new contacts at lunch and learning about their business. But they're not too busy to have lunch and yak with the same old people.

They are doing exactly what they want to be doing.

My friend Alice is a successful partner in a law firm. It wasn't easy for her. She was a single mom raising two kids at a time when female lawyers weren't promoted to partner regularly. Alice knew that she wanted to make partner because that was the way to ensure her financial future. She found ways to not let "busy" stand in her way. Was it a challenge to get out there and meet prospective clients and contacts regularly? You bet. But she didn't allow "busy" to prevent her from doing the things necessary to help her accomplish her goals.

No one is too busy to have breakfast with new contacts once or twice a week, or pick up the phone once a week to reach out to old contacts and clients. No one is too busy to attend one or two networking events a month.

But more importantly, if you knew your next job or client was waiting at that breakfast seminar you were thinking of attending, would you be too busy?

When you tell people how busy you are, it isn't upping your credibility factor, believe me. The first thing people think when you tell them how harried and busy you are is, "Gee, this person doesn't have it all together." Or "I don't know if I should hire this person. He/she is so busy. Will I get the attention I deserve?"

Busy is trite.

Ditch this excuse now. It's not doing you or your career a bit of good.

Busy is the easiest thing to be, and the least effective.

The Sneaky Truth About Inauthenticity

You may be asking yourself if all of this strategy around meeting the right people sounds a bit calculating or manipulative. Or inauthentic.

The premise of everything I've put forth in this book is here to help you be effective **and** be yourself. It's designed to guide you in developing a process that works and that fits you. But, if you really aren't interested in others and how to relate with them, none of this will make much of a difference.

Inauthenticity is very hard to hide. People tend to smell it a mile away.

Authenticity is unmistakable.

Are there are a few folks who can pull the wool over others' eyes and appear authentic? (The most diabolical example of such a person is Bernie Madoff) Certainly. But for the most part, inauthenticity brings people's guards up.

When you really are interested in others, people "get" this. They are drawn toward you.

Here are two stories, one on each side of the authenticity mirror.

A big-city insurance agency broker has been leading a networking group for years. He's a guy with a strong personality, whose mantra for the group is about giving not receiving.

One of the new members of the group had been referring business to the other members generously. He was intent on being a good contributor to his group.

This leader called the new member and commended him for his referral activity. Then he said, "I'd like us to get together for breakfast. You haven't been sending any referrals my way. I don't think you have a clear enough picture about what I do."

On the one hand, this behavior was certainly authentic: The message was "Where's mine?" (isn 't that attractive?) The message, however, was in direct conflict with his mission for the group. His actions totally repelled this new member.

The new member agreed to the breakfast but set a time limit to the meeting (restricting the possibility of relationship-building and preventing a time drain). At the breakfast, the new member told the leader he understood very well the nature of his business and that he had several insurance connections that he felt were referrable. He was pretty straight with this group leader: "I'm concerned you're going to come on too strong and insistent with my contacts and clients. We need to get to know one another better before I start referring them to you. I imagine you'd want to get to know me better too."

The last thing this new member was going to do was recommend Mr. Pushy to his revered contacts and clients. When you come from a MeMeMe perspective, people will instinctively run in the other direction.

On the flip side, we all know financial advisors have a challenge because there are many of them and people are immediately on their guard around them. They have a reputation for being overbearing and "salesy."

A respected colleague of mine recommended I network with a financial advisor. While I inwardly groaned, (nothing against financial advisors — just that it's a knee-jerk reaction after years of experiencing the above). when this colleague advises me to meet someone, I go. No questions asked because my I completely trust my colleague's people sense.

I met Mr. Financial Advisor for coffee one Friday afternoon on my way home. It was the single best surprise of a networking meeting I've ever had. This guy was smart, interested in me and what I do, generous, and anything but salesy. We have now spent the last year introducing great people to each other. These introductions have led to some remarkable opportunities for both of us. In fact, he's been responsible for my working with some excellent clients.

He is totally authentic and interested in giving opportunities to the "right" others. He's careful about who he interacts with, but comes from a totally generous and open-hearted place. As a result, people are drawn to him! He has great referral sources and clients, he earns their trust, and he does a great job for them and their businesses.

Authenticity works every time.

What If I'm An Introvert?

There are some people who find it very challenging to interact with strangers. We often categorize these people shy or introverted.

In our society (unlike other societies) being extroverted and a "people person" is revered and understood. We understand shy people or introverted people less. Sometimes we see introverts as cold or aloof.

These folks are often the most under-rated and misunderstood. If you are seen as shy or introverted, can you build "just the right network" for you? Do you have to become an extrovert to succeed?

Absolutely not. However, you will want to tailor many of these techniques to fit your style and personality.

In Thomas M. Murphy's book, *Successful Selling for Introverts*, he outlines a number of the introvert's personality characteristics and how these can be leveraged as a sales or career advantage. I suggest you read this book and do the accompanying exercises to develop your approach **in sync with your traits** vs. trying to "fix" them.

The most important attribute of the introvert that is also a huge advantage is the ability to be an excellent listener. Since this can often be a major disadvantage of the extrovert, many of whom can't stop talking and stealing the spotlight, I suggest you leverage this wonderful skill by learning to ask great probing questions, while letting your colleagues speak and share all about themselves. Your ability to listen, absorb, process, learn, and then connect the dots of your service with their needs can put you in the lead over extroverts in the business arena.

Awareness of your personality traits as advantages will be self-confidence feeders, so it is important for you to study these and learn to flip what you have previously considered limitations into benefits.

CHAPTER 6

Relate Like A Fox: Build Deep Relationships With The Right People For You & Your Business

Unlimited power may be available when two or more men coordinate their minds and deeds in a spirit of perfect harmony for the attainment of a definite purpose.
—Napoleon Hill

RELATIONSHIPS: The most misunderstood word in the language of business.

If you have a service-based business, you know that networking and building relationships is essential.

But what does that really mean? People talk about wanting to build relationships as if everyone they talk to has the same definition of what a relationship is.

The idea is to build the kind of connection with someone where you both experience interest in, respect for, and caring about supporting each other in business and personal success.

But how do you actually move from being perfect strangers to developing that rich, rewarding business relationship we are all seeking?

Let's follow the typical thread:

You meet someone at a networking or business event.

You agree to follow-up or get together afterward.

In that meeting each person is hoping a favorable result will come out of that meeting.

Let's put a pause button on the scene.

The reality is that it takes a number of meetings, touches, experiences to find out what makes that person tick, how he or she operates, whether they will make you pleased you referred him or her or mortified that you made the match.

Relationships are not made in one meeting. They evolve. It takes time to learn about another person's generosity as a business colleague.

More than once, I've referred people I've met through networking to clients and others in my network, and received reports about embarrassingly bad behavior or performance. I simply referred them too early.

Jonathan was introduced to me by a mutual colleague. He is a successful insurance broker and financial advisor. We set up an exploratory networking meeting to learn more about each other's businesses. At the time, one of my key clients was a rapidly growing professional services firm.

Over lunch, Jonathan described his approach to business as relationship-driven. He said he was all about building relationships. There was the "R" word again. Of course, I too am a relationship builder. I continued to listen.

Jonathan talked about introducing me to several of his contacts and he'd love to be introduced to the leadership of my professional service firm client.

Jonathan was a man who looked, walked, and talked top tier. He was successful, polished, and spoke the lingo.

I thought he might be a good fit for my client so I proceeded to set up a series of lunches with him and the leadership of this firm.

Over the next few months, my client had some meetings with Jonathan and some of the folks in his group, but they didn't refer any business to him. He complained about it to me. And he certainly never introduced me to any of his contacts.

What I learned from this is that Jonathan really believes he's all about building relationships, but in reality, he's about building opportunities for himself. That was the last major introduction I made to Jonathan.

Jonathan is really a delightful guy to be around. Nevertheless, the word relationship doesn't mean the same thing to him as it does to me — or others.

So how do you select people with whom it's ideal for building business relationships?

1. *Intuition:* Select people you intuitively like and respect.
2. *Business acumen:* Select people who have a solid business track record.
3. *Generosity:* Seek people who demonstrate, not just talk about, generosity and curiosity about others.
4. *Work ethic and values:* Select people who show a work ethic and values similar to yours. This is so important when you want to work on a project together or to learn about that person's ability to complete something and follow through.
5. *Top notch network:* Select people who have an excellent network and Rolodex of decision makers and influencers. This is crucial because if their network is great, yours just got a whole lot greater.

People ask me all the time "How long should it take to build a relationship in business?"

I can't tell you how long it will take because you can't hurry relationships. What I have realized is that it takes about a year to get to truly know someone — fully. You might get a really good sense of them quickly, but over a year you really get to see who they are in a variety of settings and situations. You get to see the real person.

Listen Like A Fox: Hear Opportunity

Meeting the right people and building relationships calls for a skill that is rapidly becoming almost extinct: Listening.

We are so inundated with data, communications, emails, pinging, texts, and other forms of messaging that it becomes more and more difficult to focus on what others are saying.

Moreover, we not only aren't listening in a way that we truly hear what people are saying, we are missing what they are saying "between the lines" and therefore are missing huge nuggets of opportunity.

In this chapter, I want to give you some powerful hints for how to "listen for opportunity."

The better your listening for opportunity, the better you will be at being helpful to others, upping your know/like/trust factor, and being regarded as a great connector.

How To Listen For Opportunity

What do I mean by this? Again, this is a "connect the dots" process. It means that you need to listen very carefully to what is happening in another person's business, job, career, life, and world.

A number of years ago, I scheduled a follow-up breakfast with a woman I took an instant liking to at one of my monthly networking roundtable events.

At our follow-up meeting, our conversation consisted of a lot of rapport-building personal talk, not just business. It was fun. Eventually the conversation turned to the fact that she and her team had monthly lunch and learn meetings covering a variety of themes and topics that would help her and her fellow investment banking colleagues capture more market share and business.

My ear caught "lunch and learn" so I asked her about those sessions: what was the purpose, who had requested that they have them, who attended, what were some of the topics discussed, who presented, what was the format, etc.

She told me everything. Then she "complained" that the next meeting was on her shoulders: She had to come up with a hot topic and lead the discussion.

I said, "I have a ton of content. Would it be helpful if I gave you some topics and a few group exercises for this lunch and learn?" She was obviously relieved. She thanked me profusely and said she was so happy because she was not a comfortable facilitator and hadn't done it before.

I offered to give her some tips — gratis.

And then, because I listened between the lines, I realized she really didn't want to be the presenter and that the possibility of an outside workshop leader might exist.

I offered my colleague the free content (this is another reason why it's very helpful to have articles, blog posts, webinars, and other content) and I also offered to give her some pointers for facilitation. Then I said, "If you think your firm would like to have an outside specialist speak sometime, I'd be happy to cover some topics that I'm well known for that I think would have solid value for your group."

My colleague pitched this to her boss and it turned into a series of trainings to her team in Chicago.

All of this happened because I listened between the lines, connected some dots, was generous and expected nothing in return. Then, I "softly" opened up the communication lines for a mutually beneficial opportunity.

There are very few skills that will help you more than being a great listener.

Work that listening muscle.

CHAPTER 7

How To Work The Room
Like A Fox

A T ANY EVENT, whether it's an official networking event or a fundraiser, a party or any kind of gathering, you are in the midst of a major treasure chest of opportunity. Most people leave many chips on the table. I want to show you how to avoid this giant pitfall.

How do you make the most of each and every networking event you attend?

One of the reasons people dislike networking so much is that it can be a pretty overwhelming experience:

Walking into a room filled with people, many of whom are strangers, and figuring out how to meet the right ones and navigate this environment can be seriously daunting — even for the most experienced networker.

I remember being invited to a charity fundraiser at a fantastic venue in NYC — the Copacabana. I had heard about this venue and had always wanted to see it. I was pretty jazzed about this event until I walked into the room. There were 1000 people there, the music was blaring, no one was wearing a name tag, and I didn't know a single person. Could this have been any worse? I doubt it.

Being the natural introvert that I am, and at that time I was still wet behind the ears about networking, after one drink and a couple of bad appetizers, I ran out of there. That event was a wonderful opportunity to "work the room." I just didn't know how to do it at the time.

So how can you learn to "work the room like a fox" in 3 easy steps?

Network-The-Room Like A Fox: The 3 Step Program

To really work the room with fun, ease, and effectiveness, let's chunk it down into 3 simple pieces.

> Step 1: Network Sleuthing
> Step 2: Breaking The Ice
> Step 3: The Mingle-Motion

Step 1: Be A Networking Sleuth

Whether it is a party, a networking mixer, an association conference, or a regularly-meeting networking group, you should become your own Networking 007. This means you need to learn who the attendees will be, who the members are, and learn as much as possible about their backgrounds.

Does this mean everyone? Obviously not.

However, you should find out who has registered/RSVP'd to attend.

Events or groups that publish the "who's invited" and "who's coming" lists are highly desirable. You'll probably notice that for industry conferences the event hosts will publish the companies or people who have registered. You'll also be able to see all the sponsors and the list of speakers, of course.

Are the speakers in your ideal niche market?

Are the sponsors in your ideal niche market?

If attendees are listed and published, do any of them fit your "sweet spot" as either referral sources or possible clients?

When I led a one-day workshop in NYC, I first published the titles of the people I had invited.

Then as people registered, I published the attendee list.

I offered to introduce people to the registrants they wanted to meet.

The event was sold out 10 days before the event.

When I co-hosted monthly Metro Roundtable events for professionals, primarily partners in law firms and CPA firms, we listed the registrants and had a full house each month.

People want to know who's coming before they sign up. And so do you, right? It makes complete sense.

Once you've deduced that a networking group or event is right for you and your business, you will need to properly prepare yourself before you even walk into the room.

Tips For Powerful Networking Prep

Once you know who's attending or who the members of a group are:

- ▸ Make a list of 10 people you'd like to meet at the event.
- ▸ Do a study of their LinkedIn profile and visit their website or blog.
- ▸ Ask the event host if they would email connect you prior to the event or introduce you at the event. You'd be surprised how many would like to do this so that you'll say what a great event it is.
- ▸ Extra credit: reach out to these 10 people and make a date to meet at the event or after to get to know one another better.

The better your sleuthing and preparation prior to a networking event, the better you can "work the room like a fox".

Step 2. Breaking The Ice

This is the single biggest fear-factor for people when going to networking events. How do I start a conversation with a stranger, much less someone on my ideal "want to meet you" list? How am I going to break the ice with new people?

This is the main reason people seek out people they already know at a networking event or conference. It's comfortable, familiar, and they don't have to break the ice.

This is called Networking Down.

Unfortunately, this will keep you stuck and will delay your building new relationships with the right people.

What to do?

Come armed with icebreaker questions. This is the main reason I created my tip sheet: 55 Great Icebreaker Questions (you can receive it here as my gift to you http://www.thebusinessfox.com). Have about 5 to 10 icebreaker questions in mind to ask people before you walk into any networking event.

You've already made a plan to meet certain people so you should know some of their background by this time.

For those folks, ask relevant icebreaker questions that encourage conversation. Remember, your questions should be open-ended questions, ones that will generate an ongoing conversation.

The biggest mistake made at this stage is walking over to someone, asking questions that prompt one or two word answers and then launching into a soliloquy about yourself because you're nervous and don't want an uncomfortable silence to occur.

Not to worry. The antidote to mouth-runneth-over is: *think about being curious* about this person. What do you want to know about him or her?

Ask probing, insightful questions that demonstrate real interest in your new contact.

Questions beginning with Why…?, How did…?, Tell me about…, What do you think…? open up dialogue. When…?,How long…? questions can often restrict/limit real conversation. Use my 55 Icebreaker Questions Tip Sheet to get ideas for open-ended questions you can use at networking events to be a rock-star conversation-starter.

Eventually, your colleague is going to ask about you. This is usually the right time to convey your "elevator pitch" with feeling and enthusiasm. You'll know all is going well if your colleague asks you, "Really, tell me more about that."

CASE STUDY
Larry Bodine
Editor in Chief, Lawyers.com
Asking The Right Questions To The Right Person Pays Off

I would have to say that my approach to networking is best defined as one of "no strings" — particularly for doing a favor for others without expecting one in return. I believe that paying attention to others' interests, and participating when asked to volunteer pays off in spades. It actually led to one of the best results of my career.

Networking is a long-term game, requiring patience and an openness to new possibilities, because the benefits will materialize, but not necessarily immediately.

When I had my own legal marketing consulting business, I made it a practice to make friends with people from leading companies in my own field, even if there didn't seem to be an immediate prospect of working together. One such company was Lexis Nexis. I had gotten to know several people at LexisNexis at meetings of the Legal Marketing Association. Through this networking relationship, the company eventually called me in 2010 to participate in something really quite special.

LexisNexis announced the $50,000 Ultimate Law Firm Marketing Makeover Contest, and I was invited to be a judge along with David Lat, Managing Editor of Above the Law and Carolyn Elefant, Editor of MyShingle.com. The contest gave small law firms across the United States an opportunity to win a suite of online marketing services from LexisNexis valued at $50,000.

I jumped at the chance to be part of it. The company turned to me because I had been writing a successful blog, LawMarketing Blog since 2004 (this blog attracted its 1 millionth visitor in 2012!).

Then, LexisNexis invited the judges to come to New York for the celebration dinner with the winners in early 2011.

The company reserved a private dining room at the sophisticated Beacon Restaurant in Midtown. It was filled with Vice Presidents and Senior Directors from the company but one person stood out — the charismatic CEO Phillip Livingston, (probably the tallest guy in the room), a towering figure who played football for the 1981 World Champion Raiders.

Instinctively, I situated myself close by shortly before dinner was announced, and got to sit next to him at dinner. This made it really easy to strike up a conversation with an outgoing guy wearing a Superbowl ring. One of the questions I asked him was what he thought the company should do to get the word out about LexisNexis being the best choice for marketing small law firms.

He said the company could really use someone to carry the message to lawyer groups around the country. I mentioned that in the course of advising 250 law firms on law firm marketing, I was very comfortable with public speaking. It was Kismet — being in the right place, at the right time, with the right person.

This networking conversation turned into an initial speaking tour from San Francisco, to Chicago, to Philadelphia, and also included a webinar. I co-presented with marketing experts from LexisNexis at well-attended events. But the opportunities didn't stop there.

Shortly thereafter, I got a call from a Vice President whom I had met at the dinner to come to the New Providence, NJ headquarters. At lunch he mentioned that they were looking for an editor for Lawyers.com and he invited me to have this job.

I did not hesitate. Even though I loved the independence of running my own marketing business for 11 years, it was the perfect chance to get back to my roots as a news editor. In my 20s, I had started my career at the New York Daily News and the National Law Journal. This was a shot at reporting the news on a website with 3 million unique visitors per month.

In September, 2011, I joined Lexis Nexis as Editor in Chief for Lawyers.com.

The first day I walked in to LexisNexis I felt at home. I already knew a number of people. LexisNexis felt so familiar. It was as if the moment was predestined, but it was actually the result of years of networking. I had always networked proactively and strategically. This shows how the right networking created good fortune.

I wish I could offer a mechanical method for networking, where an hour of effort produces an hour of results. But I believe that if you put your best intentions and smarts into your networking, the returns will come back to you in ways you can never imagine.

Step 3: Mingle-Motion

I call this step "dancing the room."

Isn't it a big enough challenge to get a nice conversation with an ideal contact going, and already you have to figure out how to break away to meet other people too? Ugh, right?

Imagine you have a nice conversation going, and you're building good rapport. But you have 5 other people you'd like to meet before the networking hour is over. How do you move on gracefully?

No problem.

After you've been chatting for 10 minutes (you'll start to get a feel for the 10-minute mark) you tell your conversation buddy, "You know, it's been great chatting with you. We're both here to network, mingle, and meet people. May I have your business card? How about if we take this offline and set up time to continue this further by meeting or speaking over the phone? If you have your calendar we can set it up now if you like…. Or if you don't have your calendar, I'll send you an invitation by email. It's been such a pleasure meeting you, Harry…."

That's it. It's so easy, really. Your colleague is very likely thinking about how he or she should be mingling and moving on too.

You're helping yourself and them out too!

By using these 3 easy steps you can be remarkably efficient and engaging at networking events, learn a ton about the right people, and meet more people than you ever imagined. Then, once the networking event is over, you'll use The First Half Hour technique for the perfect follow-up.

Do I Need To Be Good At Small Talk?

People tell me all the time: I hate small talk. I hate making it; I hate hearing it.

There is a time and place for small talk. Small talk is only small talk if you are making it meaningless.

If you're interested in getting to know a person, the talk is rarely small because you have a genuine interest in him or her.

That's why people dislike small talk — because it's small and meaningless.

So the answer is no, there's no need for small talk. By preparing and learning about the people you are likely to meet, you'll be asking great questions, learning important information, sharing about things that are relevant to both of you.

How is that small?

CHAPTER 8

Network Like A Fox On LinkedIn: How To Bring The Cloud To The Ground

*We have technology, finally, that for the first time in
human history allows people to really maintain rich
connections with much larger numbers of people.*
—Pierre Omidyar, eBay Founder

M Y FRIEND MICHAEL and I were talking the other day about social networking. He said: Everyone I know is talking about online networking, particularly the professional networking site, LinkedIn.

What I really want to know is: Have you ever actually landed any business by networking on LinkedIn? My answer was, "Yes."

Michael was echoing the head-scratching a lot of entrepreneurs and professionals are doing when it comes to social media.

Before I launch into addressing Michael's question and give you my take on how you can "network like a fox — online" — we need to understand how vast this topic is. Techniques you need to network strategically and successfully online could (and will probably) fill the next book.

But in this book, I'm going to give you the basics, the essentials to get started, or if you've already started, some additional strategies to ratchet up your online networking ROI — return on investment.

In order to fully answer Michael's question, we have to back up a bit and define social networking.

Michael was referring to any participation on a social networking Internet site (as of this printing the big 4 are: LinkedIn, Twitter, Facebook, and a trailing 4th is Google+).

Each of these sites require you to fill out a profile with the primary purpose of connecting with others who have filled out a profile.

Each has its approach, features and benefits.

To simplify the story:

LinkedIn is the largest online professional/business social network.

Facebook is the largest social network, starting as a social/personal community, but now has morphed into a combination of business and personal.

Twitter is a combination of personal and business, but is often used as a PR/newsworthy tool by companies and business people.

Google+ is a hybrid. It is most similar in its look/feel to Facebook but focuses on circles people can create so business and personal contacts can be kept separate.

In order to optimize social networking, you first begin with the sites you decide to participate in and then develop your strategies for how to leverage each.

You need an online networking strategy as much as, or more than, your face-to-face live networking strategy. And here are a few things to consider at the outset of our review about networking online.

- The question isn't whether or not you should use online networking, or whether face-to-face networking is better than online networking. Doubts about this have long been resolved. In this era, both kinds of networking are beneficial if not essential if you want to take advantage of all the opportunities available to you and if you want to leverage all the chips on the table.

- Networking online is really the same as face-to-face networking except that you must add one more step in order to bring the connection into a living relationship.

- In face-to-face networking, you are meeting a few people and experiencing a direct personal connection. You're operating on several sensory levels —sight, sound and touch. You can observe body language. All kinds of incoming data are being processed about a few select individuals.

- In online networking, you are able to meet many more people from a larger geographic area, but with a more superficial initial connection. In other words, online networking allows you to build a bigger network faster; a face to face network allows you to build a deeper connection with a smaller population faster. For both, you will need to spend effort and time developing a relationship once the initial connection is made.

- Online networking affords you the opportunity to connect with anyone you wish if they are profiled online (and almost everyone is today) with little or no gatekeeper interference. That's a huge advantage.

But just making connections, whether online or off, will make no difference to your business at all. This is why having more connections — friends, connections, or followers — isn't the objective. Just like with in-person networking, more of the "right" connections is the key.

Because this book is focused on business networking, I'm going to concentrate on examining a site that I believe offers you the biggest business opportunity, **LinkedIn.**

The Skinny On LinkedIn

LinkedIn is the largest professional network site available today. It started out being a gigantic online resume bank, ideal for recruiters and headhunters.

But today, almost everyone in every arena of business, professional life, or corporate life has a LinkedIn profile. LinkedIn has grown to be a powerful site and is one of the most heavily tracked sites by search engines. This means that your LinkedIn profile is almost like having your own free website. LinkedIn has free membership versions and fee-based upgrade versions.

Here are some of the features:

- Extensive profile where you can feature yourself (you can also have a separate business profile)
- Your tag line or your position
- Professional skills
- Work and business history
- Accomplishments
- Testimonials & recommendations
- Content — articles, presentations, white papers you've published
- Degrees and awards
- Leadership in groups you belong to
- Skills endorsed by your contacts

LinkedIn is continuing to add new features all the time.

How To Network Like A Fox On LinkedIn

While it's ideal to connect with your ideal target market or Grow Zone connections, you will very likely get requests to connect outside of that population. I find it beneficial to connect with many people because you never know who is connected to whom.

That being said, you can categorize these people and put them into groups. Once you are clear about your ideal niche market — both referrers and end-user clients —you can prioritize these folks in your connection base.

You can send emails to your ideal connections — sharing relevant news, information, books, tips, articles and invitations to events you think would be relevant to them.

You can invite relevant contacts to have a phone conversation if they are not in your immediate geographic area, or meet face to face if they are close in proximity.

You can connect two contacts that you think would want to meet and build a relationship.

If you begin to think of LinkedIn networking similarly to meeting people face to face with an extra step of emailing them to meet, it's not that hard to see how fast you could build an amazing and expanded "Grow Zone" of connections through LinkedIn.

Strategies For Connecting With Ideal Contacts On LinkedIn

Connecting with the ideal people for you and your business on LinkedIn takes the same strategic approach as face-to-face networking. However, on LinkedIn, the right people are categorized and searchable for you.

And now, LinkedIn's search capabilities are becoming more helpful and accurate. You can do basic and advanced searches to locate ideal contacts on LinkedIn. LinkedIn has both free and for-fee upgraded features. You can accomplish quite a bit to build a top-grade network for free.

1. Making connections

Going back to your ideal client profile or referral source profile, ask yourself what terms you should search.

Let's say that sales people are your ideal clients, but vendors in your industry are the best referral sources.

One of my clients tells me that manufacturing companies are his best/ideal clients, but the best referral sources are lawyers, book-keepers, and coaches and consultants to those kinds of companies.

How would he apply that to meeting the right people on LinkedIn?

He would make as many direct connections with manufacturing owners first.

Then he would search possible connections to business attorneys, bookkeeping companies, and coaches in his geographic area.

LinkedIn's search features allow for low level or advanced searches, so accessing the ideal kinds of people is do-able.

Once identified, invitations to connect can be extended.

2. Using LinkedIn Groups to meet the right people

LinkedIn updates and groups can be used to attract ideal new relation-ships and even people to subscribe to your email list or blog.

I'd like to share a magical story about someone who"networked like a fox" on LinkedIn, my friend Mike Muhney:

CASE STUDY
Mike Muhney
How Mike Turned A LinkedIn Group Connection Into A Million Dollars In His Business Bank Account

Mike Muhney thinks a lot about relationships — especially business ones.

He began his career at IBM and cut his teeth in sales. There is no better sales training than at IBM.

Along with Pat Sullivan, Mike co-founded the revolution-ary customer relationship management software application ACT! and transformed the way sales people build relationships with their colleagues and customers forever. At the time, there was nothing like it on the market.

Once the initial euphoria faded after he and his partner sold ACT! to Symantec, Mike found himself feeling quite adrift. Although keeping busy, nothing compared to the passion he once had with ACT! and building a business, software category, and global industry.

Too young and too filled with ideas and initiative to be doing nothing, but not knowing exactly what to do, on a whim, Mike turned to LinkedIn.

The most logical place to start, Mike thought, was with his old company, IBM. As a member of the IBM Alumni Group on LinkedIn, he started interacting on some of the discussions, and then put out to the group that he was a CRM expert and would be willing to do some consulting work.

Mike was surprised when he got a response from a gentleman based in Vienna, Austria.

After a little searching about this gentleman, Mike learned that he was the founder of a 24 year old enterprise software company that was so globally successful it rather stunned Mike that Max J. Pucher would be interested in him.

After they connected on LinkedIn, Mike learned that Max's U.S. headquarters just happened to be 8 miles from his home in the Dallas/Ft. Worth area.

He said to Mike: "I'm coming over to the States in a couple of months, why don't we meet?"

In May of 2009, Mike was thinking this relationship, developed successfully, could result in a possible role as a managing director in Max's company, ISIS-Papyrus.

To make sure he had a top-notch handle on what the company was up to and it's priorities here in America, Mike attended their 3-day users conference.

And then Mike and Max met face to face. They brought the LinkedIn "cloud to the ground". Max was really enthused about the possibility of Mike joining his organization.

But those kind of decisions take time, and the fact that it was a European company presented some cultural challenges. The position Mike thought he might be hired for never materialized.

But in the process, Max got to know, like, and trust Mike.

In Mike, Max saw a man who shared his values and the know-how from their mutual former company, IBM. And Mike also had impressive credentials having created something powerful and successful with ACT!.

This bond kept the communications going. In the meantime, Mike's creative wheels were turning.

He had always been fascinated by ideas for how to take business relationships to higher levels — face to face as well as with technology.

The germ of an idea started forming, and it started when Mike fell in love with his iPhone.

It's important to remember that ACT! software was a Microsoft-based product. So when Mike bought the first iPhone in 2007, he felt a little traitorous.

By 2009, Mike was frustrated that he had this fabulous tool, the iPhone, carried with him 24/7, but because it used an APPLE system, he no longer had the software that enabled him to create more meaningful relationships that he and 10 million others had enjoyed with the ACT! software.

They say that necessity is the mother of invention, so Mike decided in that moment to create a company again.

And, once again, as he had originally done with ACT!, he thought like a user himself.

He knew it was going to take a lot of money to make his dream of bringing the value and function of ACT! to life in a mobile version. "I'm going to need investors to make this vision a reality." he thought.

He remembered Max Pucher, his fellow ex-IBM-er, LinkedIn connection, and now good colleague.

Having stayed in touch over the months, Mike reached out to Max and said, "Max, I have this idea. What do you think about it? You might be interested in looking at it."

As Mike described his new "baby," VIPorbit, Max agreed, "I'm very interested in this".

By May 2010, Mike mapped out the plan and Max Pucher became the first investor in VIPorbit. Mike deposited Max's $1 million dollar check into the company bank account. Ultimately, Max became Mike's partner in VIPorbit and the rest is history.

Now they have completed their second round of funding and the VIPorbit customer relationship management app can be found on the iPhone, iPad and in March '13 the Mac itself.

Mike wants us to take away two key things about his networking experience:

"It is important to have credentials. But that's not enough. The real asset you have to have is being able to build rapport, relate-ability, with the right people."

It was Mike's know, like, and trust factor that cemented his relationship with Max and made him want to open his wallet to Mike.

The other piece of advice is to not to focus on selling.

And we can take one more golden nugget out of Mike's story:

> Mike put himself into a powerhouse group filled with innovators and successful people — people who were building projects and companies. When you are in the company of that caliber of people, you are more likely to have higher level conversations and opportunities.
>
> Mike's story clearly demonstrates the power of online networks like LinkedIn.
>
> Mike leveraged LinkedIn in the right way — he connected online and then brought the connection to life.
>
> And now Mike is changing the business landscape one more time. As he says, "I intend, with VIPorbit, to make ACT! look like nothing more than a very successful experiment!"

When you share update posts from your blog, or article topics you write about, and provide a web link back to these sites, you entice relevant readers to subscribe to your newsletter, blog, or updates. Thus, LinkedIn is a powerful list-building tool. It is much more powerful to grow your email contact list with relevant, interested readers. They will feel connected to you and refer their business colleagues even if they have never personally met you.

It happened to me just the other day.

I was at a live networking event. When I asked the speaker a question and told her my name, she said in front of the entire audience: Oh, Nancy Fox, I get your updates on LinkedIn. That's how I read your articles and blog posts.

The speaker and I were connected on LinkedIn.

Unbeknownst to me, she had clicked on my blog post links when I posted them on LinkedIn. Now, when we met live, she felt as though she knew me.

The entire audience now had an experience that the speaker and I were connected. I got a slew of additional blog subscriptions after the event from the audience members.

This was a perfect example of how the cloud came to the ground, how my LinkedIn connections came alive.

People ask me all the time, "Why should I connect with people I don't know?"

I am completely perplexed by this.

Isn't the objective to meet new people? My question is, unless they are marketing you and pitching at you, why wouldn't you meet new "strangers" on LinkedIn?

Their network helps you grow your network.

Some people don't want competitors to see who their connections are for fear of having clients "stolen."

First, I believe in abundance and generosity vs. the mindset of scarcity or that others will take something from me. But even if that's not your philosophy (and I heartily encourage you to rethink this), you can connect with new people and still leave your privacy settings where others cannot see your contacts. In my view, it defeats the purpose of LinkedIn's open stance. I like people to know the caliber of my contacts. It elevates my standing with others.

And the better my contacts, the more I can help others connect with high-end people. That is a win-win-win all the way around.

People who feel secure about building relationships feel comfortable and confident about having an open network on LinkedIn. The main point to take away is: err on the side of connecting with more vs. less to enhance the opportunities within your network.

And, by the way, since you will be able to see what your competitors are up to, and with whom, if you are connected to them, it goes back to the old adage: "Keep your friends close and your 'enemies' [or competitors] closer."

The rich networking opportunity on LinkedIn is demonstrated by another case, that of my colleague Mike Cobb:

CASE STUDY
Mike Cobb PhD
CEO, The InnovaNet Group
How Meeting The Right People on LinkedIn Transformed my Business

It was 2010. For eleven years I had been steadily, but ever so slowly, growing my management consulting practice. While we were doing OK, I had never found the right formula, the right strategy that would enable my business to take off. I had come to the realization that the crux of the problem was two-fold. We had no one who focused primarily on business development, so that while we were exceptional at what we did, and our clients consistently acknowledged that, we seemed constantly trying to balance driving new business and at the same time delivering unparalleled service on existing engagements. In addition, when we did focus on business development, we were stuck in what I now realize was a tradition-bound selling paradigm that focused on "pushing" our services to the marketplace and largely neglecting the power of social networking.

One of our team members had been persistent in try-ing to "bring me around" to the value of social media tools, especially LinkedIn. While I intellectually acknowledged that social media could be useful in helping us grow our business, I had not fully embraced its power, and I certainly had not committed the use of social media to practice. I gave it lip service, dabbled with LinkedIn a bit, but that was about it.

Then, in early 2010, she told me about a couple of gentlemen she had met through LinkedIn. They were running a consulting practice that offered complementary services to ours, and in many of the same market sectors that we targeted. And one of them focused exclusively on developing new business for the practice. She encouraged us to meet face-to-face, which I agreed to do.

I was initially a bit skeptical, considering how my team member had met them and the fact that she really did not know them beyond social media. But I committed to listening to them, endeavoring to understand what they were doing and where they came from, and not trying to "sell" them. We hit it off, so well, in fact, that we began working together. Then, in July of 2011, we merged the two practices into what is now The InnovaNet Group. The merger, by all accounts, has been a great success. Our growth as a combined entity has far exceeded what we would have achieved separately. Plus, I have the best partners and team members I could possibly wish for. And, at the end of the day, I owe it all to LinkedIn and the fact that one team member had the prescience and determination to push me to leverage it.

But my "aha moment" didn't stop there. Over the past year I have learned to passionately embrace social networking and to approach each new relationship with an open mind and in a spirit of "giving before receiving". The payoffs to me, both tangible and intangible, are inestimable.

The salient takeaway from my experience: If you want to "network like a fox" approach each new relationship as if the opportunities that will ensue from it are boundless and in the spirit of "giving before receiving".

I love seeing how "naysaying" about social networking turns into networking that really works.

Here are my 10 favorite ways to bring the cloud to the ground and make new business connections, and build relationships with people you've never met in person.

1. Build your LinkedIn network similarly to the way you would your face-to-face network. Begin by having a strategy for:
   ▸ Who your ideal clients are
   ▸ Who your ideal referral sources are

   On LinkedIn, search through:
   A. Contacts of people in your current connection list
   B. Groups that relate to your ideal clients, referral sources, networking colleagues
   C. Titles of people or industries relevant to your business
   D. Geographical locations, if appropriate

2. Invite targeted people to connect by sending an email message communicating what you have in common and how you relate —i.e. you both know someone, you both belong to the same group or association, you both serve the same industries.

3. Invite someone to connect and ask about their business; ask who they would like to connect with on LinkedIn.

4. Search out questions a targeted person has asked or discussed on the site. Comment or respond.

5. Invite someone you are interested in to phone, Skype, or meet you face-to-face by telling him/her you want to learn more about their business, learn how you can be a better connector on LinkedIn, or discuss ways you can both use LinkedIn to further your business objectives.

6. Start a group serving your target audience. Post relevant questions and discussions. Watch who responds and follow-up with one-to-one communications.

7. Use the 1-2-3 step process to bring LinkedIn connections to life:
   1. Search and research ideal connections.
   2. Reach out, request to connect.
   3. Warm up cool connections by requesting information and turning the request into conversation.

8. Offer to facilitate a connection between someone you know and admire with someone you have just met or connected with on LinkedIn.

9. Recommend someone you admire and are connected with as a speaker at an event. This will certainly open the door to furthering the relationship.

10. Ask someone if you can blog or Tweet about them and their work.

Sometimes people are a bit lost about how to take a connection and build it into a relationship on line. Here are a few of my most successful scripts that have helped me open up a dialogue with ideal new connections:

Sample Scripts

1. *Hi _____:*

   We haven't met personally but we work (non-competitively) with similar clients and colleagues. I'd like to learn more about you and your business. Would you be available for a brief phone call?

2. *_____ has spoken highly of you and your work. Would you like to connect on LinkedIn and perhaps speak briefly to learn more about each other's businesses?*

3. *I'd like to connect you with a colleague of mine whom, based upon what I've read in your profile, I think you'd find valuable knowing. Would you be interested in an email introduction?*

4. *We both belong to the _____ group. Would you like to connect on LinkedIn and get to know more about each other's businesses?*

5. *I read your comment in the _____ Group. I appreciated this information as it helped me with an issue I am addressing in my business. Perhaps we can speak by phone to get to know one another?*

CHAPTER 9

Networking Up:
How To Network With
Decision Makers & Big Cheeses

ONE OF THE MOST CONSISTENT complaints I hear from people about networking is not only that they aren't meeting the right people.

Time and time again, I hear people tell me they are meeting "good" people but not the actual final decision makers — the ultimate contract/check-signer, the final authority on green light vs. red light.

We've already looked at how important it is to attend the right networking events if you are going to be meeting the right people for your business. But what about if the higher-level people aren't attending networking events?

This is pretty common. However, everyone in every business arena goes somewhere, even the highest honchos, even the biggest cheeses.

But where are they congregating and how can you meet them?

I am going to give some specific suggestions for this. Nevertheless, a large portion of you will still not meet the decision makers. Why? Because you are uncomfortable with approaching people you perceive to have higher stature, and so continue to connect with people at your level or below.

A few years ago, in one of my tele-classes, I coined the phrase Networking Up. I got dozens of messages from people telling me their sagas of missed opportunities because they had Networked Down vs. Networked Up.

Here's an example of how one very determined person found a way to network up and connect with the decision-makers after hearing a lot of nos.

CASE STUDY
Anjula Acharia-Bath
CEO and Co-Founder
Entertainment Portal DesiHits.com
"Eating In The Right Places
Wins The Prize Apple"

Anjula Acharia-Bath knows how to "network like a fox." She made sure she was in the right place at the right time.

Born in the UK, and having built a successful search business in England and later in the United States, Anjula always understood how important it was to have a powerful network and Rolodex with centers of influence. Hers had a heavy concentration with successful professionals in the venture capital arena.

Ranj, her husband, loved music and had a hobby in creating podcasts of "desi" music — a fusion style mixing Eastern and Western music styles.

One day, Ranj, after playing music producer in his back bedroom, posted a "desi" podcast online. Ranj and Anjula watched with wonder as the online clicks started piling up.

Ranj added more podcasts. The clicks started skyrocketing.

Before they knew it, Anjula and Ranj started attracting the interest of not only the thousands of listeners to these desi music podcasts, but the attention of venture capitalists who smelled a potential jackpot.

Anjula, an astute business person, carefully researched the music industry and cautiously explored the venture opportunities. Fortunately, her network was filled with venture experts — but she was particularly focused on the music industry power players.

Ranj and Anjula ultimately attracted their first round of funding for www.desihits.com, enabling them to quit their jobs and focus full time on building the fledgling venture.

But Anjula and Ranj's sights were set on the big prize: a deal with Apple's iTunes.

At the time, she and Ranj were based in northern California, the backyard of Silicon Valley and Apple. Although she had tried many times to get a meeting with Apple about DesiHits, all she kept hearing was no.

Anjula knew that a lot of Apple big wigs and deal makers hung out at a restaurant in Palo Alto called Tamerine.

She knew if you want to catch a particular fish, you should go where they are swimming.

On one of the days that Anjula was lunching at Tamerine, she overheard a conversation with some men who mentioned their work with Apple.

She knew this was the moment.

Then Anjula did what only willingness to overcome fear and a huge desire will enable you to do: She started a dialogue with these folks.

"I couldn't help but overhear your conversation...." she began.

This conversation led to an introduction of Anjula to key Apple executives.

At her first meeting with Apple, Anjula closed the deal she was looking for between i-Tunes and DesiHits.

Desi Hits changed the music landscape forever by bringing Asian fusion music into the mainstream music world. They have done everything from taking Lady Gaga to India to working with the music industry's most powerful executives to bringing India's biggest bollywood star (Priyanka Chopra) to the west.

And Anjula's Networking Up led to transforming her and Ranj's lives forever.

Wanting To "Look Good" Drives People

Why do people shy away from talking to big cheeses when they have the opportunity to meet them?

It all boils down to two words: Looking good.

What I mean by that is everyone is trying to look smart enough, successful enough, educated enough, talented enough, powerful enough. Even people who say they don't care about what others think are trying to look good by thumbing their nose at society.

The converse is also true: People will do almost anything to avoid looking inexperienced, foolish, stupid, or like a failure.

It's so much easier and more comfortable to talk to people you already know and who are at your level than those who are higher up on totem pole. In other words, if we don't want to look stupid or foolish, it's safer to Network Down than Up.

Obviously that's what you should do if you want to stay stuck.

But if you really want to rev up your results, you've got to Network Up.

There are only three keys to successfully Networking Up:

1. Be in the right place with the top tier you want to meet.
2. Be prepared with what to say or ask someone in the top tier .
3. Take action and have an engaging conversation with top tier people.

That's it. Simple but not easy, you say?

Perhaps, but easier than networking with people who will not take your business or career to the right levels, don't you think?

Let's break it down then, shall we?

I. Be in the right place with the top tier for your market

Finding the right places where your top tier market is congregating is a lot like the game of connecting the dots.

We did a little of this exploring in Chapter 1 and Chapter 3. But the best way to approach this is to work backwards. Suppose you want to meet HR leaders in corporations. Where might you find them congregating?

Today, you have more opportunities for finding their "watering holes" than ever: Online and offline HR trade publications will tell you where they are meeting at conferences. LinkedIn groups will find them discussing issues online. Online HR forums will have these discussions as well. Searching LinkedIn under advanced search will pull up people who are in the HR function in a company. Then you will need to search by more criteria for your specific company and industry.

Once you find where they are congregating, you need to show up where they are.

Let's say that the top tier professionals in my target market are managing partners of law firms. They have managing partner conferences and industry association conferences. Managing partner conferences are the ideal place to directly meet these decision makers. Very often they are attending and/or speaking at a conference. And what would be really terrific? If, I too, was speaking at that conference. That would be the ultimate connection opportunity.

This is why I am always advising my clients to seek and secure speaking engagements at the events their target market attend. No strategy is more powerful for getting connected with your targeted decision makers than being a chosen speaker at events where they attend or speak.

2. Prepare yourself with smart questions and opportunities for top tier people

Once you put yourself in the same environment where your decision makers are hanging out, you still need to connect with them and engage them in some way. I know how daunting this can be but it is absolutely learnable. In fact, I was so nervous about doing this, I decided to make a game of it.

I attended the yearly kick-off event of my favorite professional business group. I had heard that traditionally this was the event that all the CEO's of top corporations actually attended. This particular group was very helpful and published the registration list prior to the event so I had a heads-up on who was likely to be there.

As a game, I picked three people I wanted to meet — heads of companies I really admired or was curious about.

One of these folks had been a leader of the NY Stock Exchange at one time. Now I know nothing about the stock market or the stock exchange. But my goal was to not only meet him but also to find a way to have a personal phone conversation with him. It was just a little challenge I gave myself.

At the cocktail hour, I searched for his name badge and found it; he was in the middle of a conversation with two other gentlemen.

It was decision time: give up and walk away or put myself on the bigger networking playing field.

I gave myself 3 seconds and then walked over (I remembered Richard Strauss's three second rule) and gently included myself in the group dynamic. They politely made room for me to join them.

A little sidebar note here: If my selected colleague had been in conversation with only one other person, I would have waited until he was either alone or with another small group. Two people speaking could be a private conversation. Three or more is usually an open conversation.

So, I said,"Hi, I'm Nancy Fox," and extended my hand. We all introduced ourselves. "May I join you?" They welcomed me in to the conversation.

Eventually, my chosen NY Stock Exchange guy turned his attention to me, and we started talking. He asked me what I did. I had crafted a version of my elevator speech to be a little more tongue in cheek for this event:

I said: "I teach lawyers who are afraid to sell how to get clients."

Mr. NY Stock Exchange chuckled. He said, "Sounds as though you have your work cut out for you. That's interesting, tell me more."

It couldn't have gone better if I had scripted it out.

Then, after a few short comments about my business, I asked him questions about his career and current professional activities.

A few moments later, I said, "I understand you've been a leader in this organization for many years. What made you become a member?" This is always a great question because it asks a person about how he or she made a choice about something; and it's not about their business but about them. Then I said, "I'd like to learn a little more and this probably isn't the best time. Would you be open to having a short phone conversation so I can learn about how you've utilized your membership over the years, and how I can better leverage mine and contribute?"

He said, "It would be my pleasure. Here's my direct extension. Contact my secretary to set up a time for us to talk."

Mission accomplished. We had an awesome conversation, and I learned some really interesting things about him and his career during our conversation.

Mostly, I proved that not only could I Network Up; I could generate a conversation with anyone at any level.

Connecting The Dots

I often mention international chambers of commerce and international networking events as ideal places to connect with higher caliber decision makers because the high-level execs attend, participate, and are accessible. Just a few examples are:

The French American Chamber of Commerce, The German American Chamber of Commerce, British American Business, and American Management Association.

Do some research to find out if chapters of these organizations exist in your area.

I'm going to list some industries that may fit your bill, but you will probably have to do some "connecting the dots" online searching for your ideal networking organizations.

Let me connect a few dots for you:

If you want to meet:
Private Equity professionals, investment bankers, lawyers, accountants, valuations specialists
Go to:
Association for Corporate Growth events

If you want to meet:
Growing entrepreneurs and business owners above the $1 million dollar level in revenue:

Go to:

Entrepreneurs Organization (EO) —this is a peer-to-peer organization

Young Presidents Organization

Women Presidents Organization

If you want to meet:

Executives and middle level managers

Go to:

American Management Association meetings

Industry-specific Management & Leadership Conferences

If you want to meet:

Owners of family owned businesses:

Go To:

Family Business Magazine Conferences

I want to introduce you now to Jason Nast, whose story about how he connected the dots helped him accomplish a remarkable goal — in under 90 days. In fact, he's such a great networker, he's got a double-great story for you.

CASE STUDY
Jason Nast
Innovator and Infomercial Master

Part I:
Why You Should Hire The Right Connector:
You and Your Business Are Worth It

Jason Nast is a guy who helps people turn their ideas into successful realities.

He connects people who have brilliant ideas to the right resources in order to take those ideas to a new level.

Back in 2005, he and a colleague developed a product called The Push Up Pro.

No, it isn't a magic brassiere.

The Push Up Pro is an upper body fitness-strengthening mechanism for men and is based on a rotating push up disc, which is now branded under different names, such as, The Perfect Push Up, and Iron Gym Push Ups.

At that time, Jason was looking to take this product to TV and needed the right contacts to do it. But not having been on the development side of infomercial products for a number of years, he was out of touch.

Back in the early 2000's body fitness for men in info-mercials was pretty much non-existent. Common thinking among the "experts" was that there wasn't a market for men in this category.

But what Jason and his team did was uniquely brilliant. Rather than asking around willy nilly, hit and miss, who could help them get their product into infomercials, they did some research. Jason searched for who had the very best contacts into infomercials. Then he hired that person.

The resource with the best contacts into this world, it turned out, was a law firm called Venable Law Firm out of Washington D.C., reputed to be the best firm specifically for TV infomercials.

Discovering this, Jason said, "Well, if I hire the top attorney there I'll also ask him to make introductions to the right people as they are processing our patent application."

This turned out to be wise thinking because they got these great introductions to the right people at the right time to take this product to market. Overcoming the assumption that "there's no market for male upper body fitness info-mercials" was largely due to Jason's persistence and the con-nections made by their attorney, Jeff Knowles, at Venable. They were able to open the right doors to entice the right people at the right time — to a market literally waiting with open arms.

But the story gets even better. Jason and his team had an idea, but they were going to have to partner with a licensee to manufacture, deliver, and distribute their fitness product. They gave themselves a 90-day window to bring their product to the consumer. Therefore, they had to put the right deals in place quickly and be ready to go.

Follow the path Jason took to search out the right person:

First, he explored who did the best infomercials with fitness products. He and his team tried to find some common denominators. The one common denominator they found was The Electronic Retailers Association. They connected to the Association through social media (which was barely in its infancy in 2005) and used email connections. It was through the Electronic Retailers Association that they found Jeff Knowles at Venable. He was active in many of the com-mittees throughout the Association. (Case in point: movers and shakers work on association committees)

Through Jeff's authority and credibility in the industry, the infomercial movers and shakers took notice of Jason's product. The attitude went from "It's not a category we want to talk about," to "How can we launch this innovative product?"

What Jason and his team didn't know was that Jeff Knowles had been positioning himself to take over as presi-dent of the Electronic Retailers Association. Their personal trusted advisor was poised to become the new head honcho of the entire industry they wanted to penetrate!

I asked Jason his thoughts on why people are so resistant to pay the money that it takes to get you where you want to go faster.

He responded with this insight: "We knew we were going to hire an intellectual property attorney anyway, but we could have hired one who was significantly less expensive. When we made the decision to hire Jeff Knowles, we knew we were not only paying for a patent but we were also paying for his connections. We knew that it was well worth the investment to hire the right guy for the right job because that guy was going to give us much more than a patent at the end of the day."

Sometimes, it really pays to pay to hire the top-notch connector in your arena. You and your business are worth it — and so are they.

Jason Nast Part 2:
How To Connect With Your Ideal Movers
and Shakers? Go Where They Are

After Jason and his team launched The Push Up Pro, they tried to connect with Kevin Harrington, who runs one of the most successful infomercial companies in the world, TV Goods. Kevin bought one of the world's most valuable Internet domain name properties, www.asseenontv.com (he paid $5 million dollars for the domain!) Kevin is a visionary with great experience, talent, and high visibility following his stint on the hugely successful TV show, Shark Tank.

Jason had been trying to reach Kevin but was unable to do so because of Kevin's stature in the industry. It wasn't an easy connection to make.

So he used his connect-the-dots muscle:

Jason knew Kevin was attending the Electronic Retailers Association Convention and was on the agenda to present an award for Direct Response Marketing. Bingo!

By this time, Jason's team had already had a great deal of success with The Push Up Pro and had created a whole new category for men's upper body fitness in infomercials.

Jason's team had been actively looking for Kevin at the convention without any success.

But then, walking down the hallway, believe it or not, Kevin found Jason.

They were walking down the same hallway at the same time, when Kevin actually came over to Jason and said, "Jason Nast, you're the guy who created that Push Up thing, right?"

He said, "Yes."

Kevin said, "You created a brand new category. That isn't done very often, so you should be congratulated."

That's how Jason met the very man he had been trying to meet, by being where he was at the exact same time.

Kevin invited Jason to his private celebration party for his purchase of asseenontv.com. There, Jason met many movers and shakers in the industry. It was a bonanza of top tier connections.

Ultimately, Jason and Kevin worked on a big project together.

Jason's words to the wise networker: "You need to connect the dots — research and think strategically, and then show up at the places your ideal people are likely to show up. Sometimes it's at a conference, where that ideal person might be a panelist, and you're asking questions. These people also go to dinner and walk back to their hotel room. Create your opportunities by being there, too."

See why learning how to scope out where you should be networking is so beneficial?

Practice searching for networking events or conferences in your area where your target "Grow Zone" market will be attending.

Who's In Your Dream Network?

If you could network with anyone in the world, who would it be? Most of us immediately cut off thoughts of meeting higher level people, thinking either it can't be done or we wouldn't know what to say to these people.

I challenge you to play big, and start Networking Up all over the place.

A client of mine (we will call him Stuart) was in business furniture sales. His business was pretty good, but he wanted to take a big leap forward. He wanted to get at least one million-dollar client by the end of the year. Up to this point, his biggest client did about half a million in volume per year.

When we looked at where he was networking, and the prospects he was meeting, the problem became clear.

"Stuart, are any of the contacts you've been networking with capable of becoming million dollar a year or more clients?"

He thought about it a minute and said, "No. None of them could ever buy at that level. They're too small."

"So, what kinds of characteristics does a company have when it is capable of buying at the million dollar level and beyond?"

We started to make a list: The companies had to be in the hundreds of millions in revenue or more; they very likely required a lot of bigger pieces of furniture with a high level of replenishment so the furniture gets highly used; and they needed multi-locations.

Bingo.

He started networking with top leaders in the hotel industry, and sourced bigger companies with multi-locations, chain operations.

By Networking Up, Stuart not only closed his first million-dollar account by the end of the year, he had a second million-dollar client on the books shortly after the first of the year.

Today it's easier than ever to meet higher level people. LinkedIn and Twitter make it easy to find and connect with people it would have been impossible to meet years ago because the gatekeepers would be a giant barrier keeping you from getting your big cheese on the phone. But today, many influencers and top brass manage their own LinkedIn and Twitter accounts, making them much more accessible.

You may also find that some very surprising people may give you access to high-powered connections.

Ruta Fox found this out a number of years ago.

CASE STUDY
Ruta Fox CEO Divinediamonds.com
Creator of The Ah Ring™
Networking My Way to A Million Dollars

After many years as a freelance writer, I knew that this career was winding down. For health and other reasons, I badly wanted to and needed to make a change.

I have a psychic in Los Angeles named Beatrice Marot. She has been a friend of mine for 30 years, and I speak to her quite often. She has given me advice about men, jobs, dating, etc. the usual things that single girls want to know about. We would often do a "reading" where I would get my tarot cards read. I would always take notes when I got a reading and then I would try to follow the advice that was laid out before me. But I never knew that my connection to my psychic would also be the networking connection of my life.

I needed to come up with a new way to make a living. I used to sit on the couch each day and pray for divine wisdom and intervention. And amazingly, one day, I did come up with an idea. I created a ring called The Ah Ring, the first and only diamond ring designed for single women to buy for themselves. The Ah stands for **A, available** and **H, happy** and it's designed to be worn on the pinkie. I figured there were diamond wedding rings and engagement rings, why wasn't there a diamond ring single women could wear? A friend of mine saw the one I was wearing, and asked me where she could get one.

Soon, I was going all over town in NYC and selling them to my girlfriends. Then, Beatrice the psychic told me to call one of her contacts Michelle Oliver, who had gotten a job working at Oprah's O Magazine.

O Magazine had just launched in 2001, and it was THE place for magazine people to work. People were going crazy to work there. Michelle had gotten the job by a total fluke. She had been asked to work there after a chance conversation with someone on the subway...too crazy. (talk about "you never know networking!") So many people were going after jobs there, but somehow she was in the right place at the right time.

I contacted Michelle telling her I had been referred to her by Beatrice, and told her how I had designed this cute diamond pinkie ring that everyone loved. She told me she had just been looking for one at Cartier, but they were way too expensive — but she would love to see mine and invited me to come over the next day.

I couldn't believe I had gotten the perfect connection into O Magazine.

I walked over and went up to O Magazine on the 38th floor. I got to the office and showed Michelle my Ah Ring and she took out several hundred dollars and bought a ring right there on the spot. Then, she called in the other girls in the office... the Accessories Editor and the Style Director of the magazine. They both proceeded to buy rings too. I was so excited. I walked home ten feet in the air that day with a big wad of cash in my pocket.

The next morning, the phone rang and I answered. A women said, "This is Frances, I'm an editor at O Magazine. We Fed Exed your Ah Ring press package to Oprah overnight, and she wants The Ah Ring to be featured on the O List."

I had actually only sold 20 Ah Rings for cash to a few girlfriends and been hand delivering them all over town. Now, here was my "brass ring", my chance to be featured in the most successful magazine launch in history, O Magazine, with a circulation of three million. I wasn't even a real business yet. But I put everything together in six weeks and suddenly I was. Everyone knows what happens when Oprah puts her stamp of approval on a product — "The Oprah Effect!" It ultimately turned into a million dollar idea. And it happened, all due to networking with the right people! Obviously my psychic knew the right people and now I do too.

CHAPTER 10

How To Build An A-List Network By Writing A Book

Work smarter, not harder.
—Carl Barks

No time to network. I hear this all the time.

No time to blog, market, get speaking assignments either.

And there is definitely no time to write a book.

I'm just too busy trying to find clients and service the ones I have.

Would you like to know how to build that A-List network, get connected to decision makers and complete a project, find great leads, build visibility — all at the same time?

It sounds too good to be true, doesn't it?

Well, I didn't say it wouldn't take some really big effort, but I can tell you it is an absolutely effective way of expanding your sphere of influence with ideal people, and if done right, a powerful lead generation method at the same time.

This is the advice I gave to a client of mine.

Robert wanted to meet high level decision makers in companies that had between hundreds of thousands to millions of names in their databases. He owns a database consulting business and his ideal clients are major corporations and financial institutions with huge databases.

Getting in front of these decision makers is, as you can imagine, a very big challenge.

Robert also had a deep desire to write a book about the secrets to success buried in databases, and how businesses could leap forward if they had more ways of leveraging this information.

So I asked Robert why he couldn't do both at the same time — meet decision makers and write a book.

After he stared at me blankly, I asked him to make a list of the company leaders he'd love to meet and talk with as potential clients.

I then asked him to make a list of leaders and experts that would be ideal to be interviewed for the book.

When he looked at both lists, he smiled. There were many people on both lists!

Robert did proceed with interviewing leaders for his book. Almost every person he asked to interview for his book said yes. He not only had no difficulty getting past gatekeepers, he was warmly welcomed, built new relationships with these decision makers, and cultivated a number of ideal prospects, a number of whom became new clients.

Here are 5 ways to ramp up your visibility, influence and connect with influencers and decision-makers simultaneously:

I. Write a book

Interview top experts on a needed topic for your markets. Now your interviewees are not only giving you the content for your book, you've gotten past the gatekeeper and you have a direct connection to the decision maker.

Many people are dying to write a book, but they don't believe they have the time.

Many people would love to build a high-level network, but they don't believe they have the time.

And many people would love to get in front of more decision makers but don't see how.

I see this as the perfect opportunity to leverage one objective off the others.

The easiest and most effective way is to write a book by interviewing the very people you'd like to have as clients. Then, you can self-publish it and feature these interviews as the content of the book. You'll be killing two birds with one stone and have a book to sell to boot.

2. Feature Well-Known Bloggers

Want to build your blog recognition factor faster? Ask a successful blogger if you can feature their work on your blog and give them credit. Cultivating top blogging content and compiling it makes for great blog content but also will boost visibility for your blog.

3. Podcasts — Host A Radio Show or Online TV Show

Want to meet A-Listers? Ask if you can interview them on your online radio show (Blog Talk Radio) or use the podcast audio link in your newsletter, on your website, or on your You Tube TV Channel.

Dan Toombs is the founder of Fast Firms. It's a legal marketing consultancy based in Australia.

Dan wisely realized that many lawyers and law firms want visibility and greater recognition online. He created a podcast series by interviewing dozens of experts in the legal marketing field. It gave Dan added credibility, visibility, and access to ideal prospective clients. It also helped each of the people he interviewed get additional visibility.

4. Host a Panel Discussion with A-Listers

A-listers love being asked to be on panel discussions because it requires less work than planning a speaking engagement, particularly when they will be on the dais with other A-listers.

How do you get the first A-lister to say yes?

- ▸ You can ask someone you know who is a top dog to be the first "yes."
- ▸ You can tell the candidates about the other people you are inviting to be on the panel so they know the caliber of those they will be hanging around with.
- ▸ You can ask an A-lister who is in the middle of promoting a book because they always want as much publicity as possible.

Here's an example where this last approach paid off beautifully:

My colleague and I wanted to host a professional service firm Managing Partner event so we could be in front of our top tier market. We decided to create a Managing Partner panel discussion and cocktail party entitled "The Art Of The Merge" because mergers are a hot topic in professional services.

First, we enticed a couple of Managing Partners to be on the panel.

We needed a big name to ensure that these high-level, busy Managing Partners would actually show up.

At the time, Charlie Gasparino of CNBC had just written a book and was on the promotion circuit. He agreed to moderate the panel discussion on "The Art Of The Merge" at this event. Instead of a moderator's fee, Charlie agreed to do the gig if we bought some books. We did and gave each attendee a signed copy.

We had a goal of 40 MPs. We had 100% registration, and 39 out of 40 showed up. It was a massive success. We had sponsors, so the event was paid for, and we got to hang out with top law and accounting firm leaders in one fell swoop.

Then after the event we followed up with each of them.

A-List networking building on steroids.

Was it a lot of work? You bet. But so much more prestigious and effective than trying to cold call and meet them one by one

5. Hosting an Event to Build Your A-List Network

A number of years ago, I used these exact strategies to host a top-tier professional women's networking event. I wanted a featured "celeb" to be a sponsor and registration draw. Carolyn Kepcher (you may remember the "blond in the boardroom" of *The Apprentice)* was just launching a new website and agreed to come and receive a "She Means Business Award" at my event. I invited Links of London to be a featured sponsor, and they provided and presented Carolyn with the award — their most popular bracelet.

Carolyn said a few words about her new project, *The Apprentice,* and women's networking. Links of London talked about supporting women business owners. It was a win, win, win all the way around.

Because of Carolyn's appearance, a reporter from the *Wall Street Journal* attended and gave us coverage for the event, as did representatives from two professional services publications.

Months later, Carolyn began writing for the *Daily News* and interviewed and quoted me in one of her articles.

This is a perfect example of how you can explode your A-List network in one fell swoop by hosting an event.

This savvy strategy also worked very successfully for Gordon Epstein. Take a look at how hosting events has paid off in spades for a guy who started out rather unsure of himself but turned that around in a very rewarding way.

CASE STUDY
Gordon Einstein
Founder
AdaptiveSky.com

Geek Lawyer Grows Into Successful Life Of The Party — And Grows His Business TOO

How did a basic business lawyer go from being a shy guy to becoming a local networking celebrity and building his business at the same time?

Gordon Einstein began his career rather unremarkably: Respected law school, practiced estate and business law for a few years, not having much fun.

What interested him were the businesses of some his clients, many of whom were (this being the early 2000's) dot coms and techie companies.

On sheer intuition and hunger for something new, Gordon decided to switch career gears.

He had always liked technology — he was an early adopter of Apple, games and all things techie —so he threw himself into making the career shift into technology and cloud consulting.

He started off small, training people with their home computers, then expanding into their office systems. Over time (a long time) the systems kept getting larger and larger.

All the while, Gordon was very much a shy, behind the scenes kind of guy.

This is common with tech-type people — falling more on the introvert vs. the extrovert side of the personality scale.

Wisely, as the "cloud" became the future of data and interactivity management, Gordon leveraged his relationships from his legal days and began designing and developing unique cloud data systems for law firms and other professional firms.

But, being this shy guy, and wanting to speed up his business results, Gordon knew he'd have to "get out there more" if he wanted to grow.

So he joined a couple of local networking groups that catered to the legal market.

Because his story, "the lawyer who switched careers," was unusual, it helped him meet lots of people and helped him build those intangible but oh-so-crucial face-to-face communication skills.

In the beginning, Gordon found networking nerve-wracking. He grew up shy, socially insecure, never cracking a single joke until he was a freshman in college.

The first time he inadvertently cracked a joke and people laughed, it was like a light went on in Gordon's world.

He started to open up to people.

He started to not let his supreme nervousness in networking groups stop him from getting up and speaking about his services and their benefits.

He found that as he became more competent, he grew in confidence.

A stroke of intuition and impulsiveness prompted something transformational — for Gordon, but for hundreds around him as well.

Gordon decided to take his networking into something he'd personally feel more comfortable with: social happy hours.

The formality of most networking events were always out of Gordon's comfort zone, so he decided to take networking into the fun zone.

At first, he just invited a few colleagues to informal happy hours.

To up the fun factor and underscore the informality of his connecting style, he started doing clever invitation themes.

It began with themes like:

No Name Tag Happy Hour

He built a website including rhymed, hyperlinked invitations, things with political commentary, even going so far as to write limericks in his invitations.

(Maybe we could call Gordon Einstein the "limerick lawyer?")

These where not your garden variety networking event invites.

These had some pop to them, they had humor in them.

Here was something fresh and invigorating — people didn't groan at the invitations, they looked forward to them.

Gordon, out of his own need, tapped into something quite unexpected: the need many people have for personalizing their way to network and connect.

Next, thinking of the most un-businessy-name he could come up with for a networking event, Gordon launched Happy Hour Mafia. Then he started numbering these events, letting people know that these were a series they could look forward to.

Happy Hour Mafia is now at Happy Hour Mafia #40.

Gordon still marvels at how this effort has mushroomed, grown and helped him grow his business and the businesses of the many who frequent the Happy Hour Mafia shindigs.

The financial benefits also showed up.

Gordon's events were so well attended that the restaurant locations started providing discounted food and drinks to the attendees. And then in another stroke of genius,

Gordon didn't take a cut of the revenues generated — he donated these proceeds to charity.

It built good will and respect among the attendees, the venues were happy with the business and Gordon's costs were covered. Win–Win–Win.

The events foster relationship building so business opportunities just naturally flow.

Gordon revels in the dozens of emails and thank you's from people getting business out of the fun at Happy Hour Mafia nights.

Gordon says that in launching something that was completely out of his comfort zone, people's lives were changed. Happy Hour Mafia has led to a couple of marriages and families being started.

Gordon shares an important piece of advice for those who are thinking of hosting their own events to network and grow in business:

"Whoever you are, you need to approach it in a way that is true to who you are. Trying to do this like someone else does it, if it's not authentic to you, will certainly flop. It's great to stretch your boundaries, it's another thing to try to be someone else."

But Gordon did stretch out of his comfort zone, all the while being true to his spirit and love of fun.

CHAPTER 11

Building The Right Network Within Your Own Company

The richest soil is often right in your own backyard.
—Anonymous

WHETHER YOU ARE working in a company or organization, or are looking to be working within one again, the principles of networking to build the right internal network will make the difference between mediocre accomplishments and outstanding ones.

Even when you are working within a company, you must always be networking.

I know you think that if you have a job, there's no real need to network. Nothing could be more short-sighted.

I've made this error and paid a very big career price for it. I watch many people make this same error.

Due to the collapse of the economy in 2009 and the landslide of lost jobs, we now have millions and millions of former executives, specialists, sales people, and professionals who are talented, smart, experienced, successful, influential people looking for work after years of inattention to network-building.

The result of this arrogance and laziness (yes, you heard me, it was lazy and arrogant to think that because you had a job you didn't really need to get out there and nurture your network) is that we have hordes of people desperately trying to build a productive network fast to find opportunity and land their next job.

While there are many more tools and outlets today that didn't exist years ago (online resume sites, and of course LinkedIn) remember that there are also many millions of people trying to leverage these very same tools at the same time.

Harvey Mackay, the author of one of my favorite books on networking, said, "Dig Your Well Before You're Thirsty."

In other words: Always Be Networking

To be really smart about networking before you are desperate to build a network, the place to start is right in your own professional backyard.

Networking Up Within Your Company

Most companies are hierarchal pyramids. You have a CEO, then one step down is the President, then the Exec VP, the VPs, the Directors or Managers, the Coordinators, Team Leaders, Assistants, and so on.

The titles may change; the structure is still a pyramid.

The lower on the pyramid you are, the less influence you have on the organization as a whole. Trying to capture the attention of the President or CEO is a big challenge unless you're in a small company with lots of personal interaction at all levels.

I've worked in Fortune 100 companies, mid-sized companies, and small companies, in the U.S. and internationally. My clients have ranged from huge corporations to professional service firms of 20 people or less.

In every single case, the relationships and connections of the people within each organization had more to do with the professional trajectory of the individual employees than their smarts or how effective they are.

Perhaps this is why Steve Job's most revolutionary years were when he didn't have to worry about pleasing the higher ups — he was the higher up and could create and do things his way.

For most of us, the power of building a network of internal influencers can make or break our careers.

As you have by now come to expect, I recommend you have a Networking Up strategy. While this may appear calculating, in my experience I've found having a thoughtful, strategic approach will save you time and disappointment in the long run.

Circles Of Influence

As I've said before, not all networks are created equal. (Sorry to be a nag, but repetition helps you remember).

This is why it's not about how big your network is; it's about the quality of your network.

Most people have on average about 200 people in their immediate network (here I am referring to people you interact with directly, personally, whether frequently or infrequently.) Today, this number might be substantially bigger through social media connections, but for the purposes of this discussion, I am referring to off-line contacts.

In your organization, whether it has 20, 200, or 20000 employees, there are still circles of influence.

Key Influencers

Key influencers are the decision makers. This is the inner circle of people who decide where the ship is going and who will be manning the key levers of the ship as it navigates the seas. Key influencers only invite trusted colleagues into the inner circle. These are the people they believe will have their back and help them further their objective and mission. Key influencers generally hang out with other key influencers because they know that other influencers have access to superior resources and contacts in high places. These relationships increase the odds of accomplishing their objectives.

Megaphones

The Megaphones are the magnifiers, the amplifiers of the corporate message. They have a voice that is heard and listened to by the key influencers.

Executers

Executers carry out the message of the Megaphones. For any of their voices to be heard, they will have to be filtered through the Megaphones, and only periodically heard by Key Influencers.

The objective is to develop as many solid relationships with Key Influencers in your organization as possible.

Know The Right People

Very early in my career, I took a job in a women's underwear company.

My dad was in the women's fashion industry. He was a designer with some of the best-known designers in the industry — such as Calvin Klein, Ralph Lauren, etc.

At one of the seasonal fashion shows, he met a man who was the Vice President of Advertising for a women's underwear company in Los Angeles. It was a coincidence that this man was at a fashion show. He knew all the editors of the fashion magazines, and they invited him to all the top shows.

It was also a coincidence that this man's company was in Los Angeles (which is where I was living at the time) because most of the women's underwear industry was based in New York City.

My father, trying to help me advance my career, begged me to call his advertising friend.

Being young and really inexperienced in the ways of the business world, I wasn't sure what I would have to say to my dad's friend if I did call.

But I really needed to get out of my low-paying, going-nowhere job at an insurance company so out of desperation and to get my father off my back, I called his friend.

As hard as that phone call was to make, that phone call led to my getting a job as a sales associate for The Olga Company, a women's intimate apparel company, working for a top-ranked Regional Sales Manager.

After a couple of years proving myself at the sales level, I realized I loved the product and wanted to work in Product Development. Because my boss (a Megaphone) had great favor with the VP of Sales, he endorsed me with the VP and within in 2 months I was given a product development assistant's position. That's how my career as a product and marketing executive was launched. Without the endorsement of my boss (a Megaphone) I would never have landed an interview with the VP of Sales (a Key Influencer) who was in the inner circle of the founders of the company.

How To Stand Out (In A Good Way) With Big Cheeses When You Are A Little Cheese

CASE STUDY
Entry Level Eric

Eric is an ambitious young guy working in a Fortune 500 company. But he's in an entry-level position.

It's very challenging to build a network of Key Influencers when you are a bottom-rung worker in a huge organization.

There are so many layers to get through to be noticed and connected to the Key Influencers.

But Eric is not the kind of guy to wait around for others to help him advance. He decided to take destiny into his own hands — and get to the big cheeses.

Eric's Clever Connecting Strategy:

Eric's company had a program called "lunch and learns". Lunch and learns within companies are usually one-hour sessions where people can hear presentations on a variety of topics. It's usually very informal — people bring their lunch, eat it while they are enjoying the presentation, and they can show up at will.

Well, Eric, who was in the marketing department, created a big show. He'd do these outrageous presentations. In the beginning, just his friends and fellow co-workers would show up to support him. But he was so creative and innovative that the word started to spread. Soon, his presentations were SRO, and you had to pre-register to get a seat.

The word eventually reached the ears of some company Megaphones and Key Influencers. Eric started to meet the Key Influencers in his company. They were so taken with Eric's ingenuity and initiative, he was invited to make his presentations to the senior management of the company,

Eric's accomplished a key objective in a relatively short period of time — to get noticed in a positive way by the big cheeses in his company. He didn't let his lower stature on the totem pole or small thinking get in the way of being noticed.

Moral of the story: Don't let being a little cheese stop you from letting the big cheeses see your brilliance.

How To Expand Your Influence In Other
Departments In Your Company

Just as I wanted to move from Sales into Product Development in my earlier years in the women's underwear business, many professionals I speak to want to move to other departments in their companies as well.

Most companies don't encourage this, especially if you're doing a great job. Why lose a good person, right?

That was Robert's dilemma.

Robert is a mid-level executive in the television industry. He came to me with a serious career issue: he had a negative attitude, he hated his job, and he wanted to move into the more strategic area of television programming. (He was currently working in operations). The timing for Robert was crucial because he was moving into his mid-30's. Television is a very youth-oriented industry, and career trajectory is usually set for an employee by his or her mid to late 20's.

So Robert and I got to work.

First, we worked on an attitude adjustment. This was an essential foundational ingredient if he wanted to have the big cheeses see him differently. He took on changing his attitude and behavior around his staff, his co-workers, and his boss. People around him started to notice a major shift. That prompted two important changes: in a 6-week period of time, he was promoted (with a nice salary increase) and then he was invited to join the monthly divisional strategy team.

He continued to represent operations, but being part of this divisional strategy team gave him visibility and direct access to a Key Influencer, the head of television programming.

Boom.

This key influencer liked what Robert was contributing in the meetings. He took a shine to Robert and they started to build a relationship.

It's very unusual for a mid-level manager to move from one department to another in a company without the strong endorsement of a Key Influencer.

Robert's key to unlock this possibility was being in front of the right Key Influencer every month and demonstrating big value.

Now, he has an opportunity to build a relationship and credibility with the exact right Key Influencer who has the ability to move him from one area to his dream division.

Bring Your A-Game To Play With The Big Cheeses

As a young executive in a big company, I didn't know anything about networking when I started out. But, like Eric, I instinctively knew I had to play with the big players in order to get noticed and ultimately promoted.

It called for some pretty gutsy moves on my part.

One of the best jobs I ever had was at a division of Warnaco as a Product Manager.

The senior management of this organization (it was about $100 million in revenue at the time, with hundreds of employees all over the world) was a great group of leaders.

At first, I had a boss who was very powerful but not well respected. He was a big cheese but not a Key Influencer. Within a year he was out.

But my new boss was both influential as well as powerful. And in many respects, she was a mentor to me. After a while, she invited me to audit (not participate in) the senior monthly Executive Committee Meetings. This was an excellent opportunity to watch the inner workings of the company, and to hear how all the strategic decisions were being made and by whom. I heard the financial reviews and discussions and observed the politics within top management. I loved this.

It was outstanding as a new middle level executive to be in the room with the big honchos and observe how they made their decisions.

But there was another world that was not so easy to break into.

The Executive Lunch Table.

Every day, all the senior executives sat at the same table at lunch. The president and all the vice presidents, except for my boss, sat and had lunch together. All the executives, except for my boss, were men.

I knew that to break through that glass ceiling I had to have more "social" time with the "big boys."

This company was a good old boy culture, so breaking into the Executive Lunch Table was not just breaking through the glass ceiling, it was breaking through the gender barrier.

The first day I brought my lunch tray over to that table was terrifying. I didn't know if they'd tell me to leave or not.

Truth be told, I was quaking in my high heels, and they looked at me with mortified expressions when I sat myself down with them.

What was worse was that the lunch conversation revolved around sports, specifically football. I knew absolutely nothing about football, nor did I want to know anything about it. So I sat there like a lump and listened more than interacted.

For months I forced myself to sit at the Executive Lunch Table three times a week. The men got used to my being there, and they eventually looped me into the conversation. My lateral colleagues were stunned, yet also a little jealous and annoyed with me. They thought I was acting too big for my britches.

I did get my first big promotion in this company, and it led me to a bigger job and bigger visibility in my industry, along with more money.

But the bigger lesson was how to feel the fear about networking up with the big cheeses and doing it anyway.

When I think back about the kind of cojones it took for that 30-something kid to push her way into rarefied air in the company, I realize how determined I was. I also see that ignorance was bliss.

But I do know this: Networking Up is the only way to play the game if you want to advance, progress, and accomplish your goals and dreams.

Help Make Big Cheeses Look Good

My cousin Daniel is one of the most unstoppable people I know. There's no question he is super smart. But he still started out as a shy kid, feeling like a misfit. Nevertheless, he didn't let his past dictate his future.

When you have a big WHY, you can change yourself, your life, your results. Daniel is proof of the pudding.

Daniel did not go to college. He wanted to see the world. He began by working for Club Med as a chef. He taught himself how to cook, and cooked with their best chefs all over the world. Then Daniel decided he needed to work in a 3-star Michelin restaurant in France as a way to ratchet up his culinary skills and demonstrate to employers he could cook with the best. Even though Daniel didn't have a top culinary school degree (or a culinary degree at all, for that matter) he networked and talked his way into an interview at 3-star Michelin rated restaurant George Blanc in Lyons, France. He didn't speak fluid French (a giant mark against him) but he wouldn't take no for an answer and proved to the executive chef that he would be an asset to the restaurant. He learned to speak French fluently so he could communicate with his co-workers.

Daniel worked for George Blanc for 2 years and was like a giant sponge. He cut his teeth on French culinary skills and how to work in a top tier French kitchen. Can you imagine the ribbing he took from the other top-trained French chefs in the kitchen?

Eventually, Daniel parlayed that experience into a sous chef position with a top cruise line.

He was so talented and hardworking and his people skills were so good that he leap-frogged over more senior culinary staff into an Executive Chef position, an officer of the cruise line, in under a year!

As amazing an accomplishment as this was, Daniel wanted to be recognized by the Key Influencers of the corporation.

He strategically knew what the biggest pain point at this level was: how to reduce costs, increase profits while maintaining the highest culinary quality. He knew that if he gave corporate leaders really valuable ideas for increasing profits/reducing costs, it would make them look good.

On his own time (and there was practically none of this —if you've ever worked on a cruise ship you know it's a 7-day a week 18 hours-a-day responsibility) Daniel put together a knockout presentation on cost cutting and quality enhancing for the cruise line.

He delivered it to the big honchos in the corporation. His objective: Give off-the-charts value, above and beyond what was expected of him, and be noticed by Key Influencers.

Daniel's approach took initiative, creative and strategic thinking, willingness to do more work than he was officially getting paid for, and a huge WHY.

A little note here: Daniel didn't do these things just to get noticed; he really believes in doing high quality work. He also believes in high quality networking.

Daniel is now connected to some of the most senior execs in the corporation. These people are on the boards of some of the biggest companies in the world. Daniel is the ultimate Networking Up master. He knows that one day it's likely he's going to want to be working at a top company outside of the culinary world. And he will now know some excellent Key Influencers to help him make this transition.

5 Strategies For How To Network Up With Big Cheeses In Your Company — Even Though You're A Mini Cheese:

1. Stand out by going above and beyond the call of duty.
2. Work for the Megaphones in the company — the ones who have clout with the Key Influencers.

3. Create exceptional value to your company/Make Key Influencers look good.
4. Hang with the big cheeses —even when you're not invited.
5. Find a way to work on committees with the big cheeses.

CHAPTER 12

Have The Right Interests, Hobbies, And Activities — Upgrade Your Network

There are rich teams, and there are poor teams...
—Billy Beane, Moneyball

I'LL NEVER FORGET the story Keith Ferrazzi tells about connecting with a conference speaker in the men's room.

Keith is the author of one of my favorite books, *Never Eat Alone*, and is often billed as America's most well-connected man. He writes about attending a conference where he wanted to meet one of the speakers. Keith had done his due diligence on this person, researched his background, and learned he had something in common with this speaker: they both were avid runners.

After the speaker's presentation, there was a big crowd around him. Keith patiently waited and watched.

Instead of battling the crowd that waits to meet the speaker at the front of the room, Keith trailed the speaker into the men's room. As they were both washing up, Keith complimented the speaker on his presentation and then moved the conversation onto their common love of running.

That conversation led them to make a running date together!

How many of us would take that kind of initiative to connect with just the right person, to "network like a fox." That's pretty foxy connecting in my book. Was it bold and did it take chutzpah? Absolutely — but look at how it paid off.

Are there certain hobbies, interests and activities that lend themselves to more productive, lucrative networking?

Like everything else when it comes to successful networking, it has to be grounded in authenticity for this kind of networking and relationship-building to thrive. You can't pretend to love art to connect with a big cheese in the art world, or love tennis to meet a big wig who also loves tennis.

Unfortunately, many do take on this b.s. kind of behavior. But real relationships that flourish long term are based on spreading what you love and are passionate about into all areas of your life.

I love sports success analogies, so I study sports personalities for lessons. This is a passion of mine. It's authentic and my conversations with anyone who loves sports and is also successful feels natural, effortless.

This wouldn't be the same if I were trying to talk about my passion about gardening. I like to look at flowers, but I'd be bored silly talking about plant fertilizer and seeds, and watering techniques.

So what are your interests, hobbies, activities?

What do you like to read about? What movies do you enjoy?

Sometimes we don't even realize that our interests outside of work can provide leverage in business networking settings.

I was watching an old movie on Turner Classic Movies (TCM Channel) recently. During one of the commercials I saw an ad for the TCM cruise vacation. It's a week-long cruise with the host of the channel and some veteran actors and stars. During the cruise a core of these movie mavens invite guests to watch and discuss classic films with them.

I thought: I bet that's going to be a fantastic networking opportunity and a built-in opportunity for common conversation and icebreakers.

One of my clients runs a property and casualty insurance firm. Their clients are all high net worth individuals with lots of expensive property and toys to insure.

Their best sales rep started his career in the construction industry. He is a total golf nut and spends every possible moment on the course. Brilliantly, he combined his love of golf and his business. He invited every single construction executive and business owner he knew to play golf. Then they invited their other construction industry friends to play with him too. Over the years, this sales rep built his entire multi-million dollar business strictly on the golf course. Because golf provides a relationship-building experience, it's fun, and offers a no-selling atmosphere, his clients easily came on board. That's a home run strategy. Or should I say hole in one strategy.

If we use a 'connect the dots' approach to networking, what are your passions and interests?

Where might your target audience be congregating on a personal basis? On the golf course, on the tennis court, at the soccer field for their kids?

My dentist loves baseball and coaches teens in baseball. He has coached the kids of celebrities and through this has been to Wayne Gretsky's house and to the homes of other celebs and honchos.

OK, you're not into sports? No problem.

It's not only about sports, although sports can be a great way to connect.

There are conferences for science fiction, comic books (a client of mind collects vintage comic books) cooking and wine and music.

Do you play a musical instrument? Do you love reading? Book clubs are fabulous ways to meet and connect with great people.

Connecting with people around mutual interests doesn't have to be at conferences.

Through the miracle of the Internet, bringing those who love what you love together became a click away through MeetUp.com

If you like dancing, music, books, movies, wine, want to network with British people, teachers, travelers…go to meetup.com. Every mutual interest imaginable is searchable locally, so you can find people with common interests right in your neck of the woods.

Some Interests Are More Lucrative Than Others

I'm sorry to say this but it's true: some interests will connect you with more high-level decision makers than others.

If you want to meet leaders and decision makers, you are more likely to meet them at events, locations, and organizations that are more affluent and influential.

Yacht clubs will have more successful people than community recreation clubs.

Fundraisers will have more affluent donors than Chamber of Commerce events.

If you're interested in golf you are more likely to interact with decision makers and wealthy people at golf clubs where it is more expensive to play than public courses.

How do you attend the events where the affluent gather when you don't have the means yet? This is where having connections can make the difference.

When you have friends who have friends in higher places, you will begin to get invitations to more affluent locations, events and watering holes where the decision makers are congregating.

This why our parents told us when we were kids: ***Who you are is who you hang around with.***

Connecting The Dots

Here are some examples of upscale interests and how to network like a fox to find your influencers, decision makers and big cheeses:

Golf . . . . Golf clubs, tournaments

Tennis . . . . Tennis clubs, tournaments

Charities . . . . Fundraisers, sitting on boards of charities you feel passionate about

Art collecting . . . . Exhibits, auctions

Boating . . . . Yacht clubs

Luxury Travel. . . . . Cruises, airline skyclubs

Wine . . . . Wine tastings, wine clubs

Cars . . . . Luxury auto shows

In 2012, the Monterey Motor Week sold $260 million in luxury cars, up from $196 million the year before!

Designer Fashion Shows . . . . . . Fashion week shows

Dog Shows . . . . Westminster dog show and other dog competitions, dog rescue volunteer groups

Cooking & Food . . . . Cooking clubs — baking, international cooking lessons, fancy food shows

Antiques . . . . Auctions

Horses . . . . Equestrian shows and clubs

Motorcycling . . . . Collections and riding groups

Diving . . . . Group diving trips

Poker . . . . poker championships and conferences

Running and extreme sports . . . running and marathon clubs, extreme sports clubs

Start leveraging not only your business interests but your personal interests in order to upgrade your network and opportunities.

CHAPTER 13

Follow-Up Like A Fox: How To Turn Follow-Up Into Your Favorite Part Of Networking

Do not wait to strike till the iron is hot;
but make it hot by striking.
—William B. Sprague

So you've gone to the networking event, or made a new contact on the airplane, or connected with someone at a conference.

Now what?

I've gone to hundreds of networking events and it is a blue moon when people follow-up with me. In almost 95% of the cases, I'm the follower-upper.

What do you think that tells us about why people are so frustrated by the results they are getting, or actually not getting, through their networking efforts?

That's one of the reasons networking businesses like BNI, Provisors, and many others have enforced structures of follow-up meetings —to ensure that people actually do something productive **after** the networking event.

Left to their own devices, most people put the business cards in a drawer and get busy with putting out the next fire.

To ramp up your networking ROI, you've got to amp up your follow-up.

But just as I don't want you to just rush out there and network any old way, I don't recommend you follow-up willy nilly, hit and miss. You can and should follow-up smarter and more strategically.

Let me explain with a short story:

I met a woman at a seminar. She was between jobs but I followed up with her after the seminar.

It so happened that her husband was the president of a major association. He was looking for a business coach for him and his staff. She was so impressed that I followed up with her, she introduced me and recommended me to her husband.

Following up with this woman turned into an eighteen-month training and coaching assignment with the entire staff of the Toy Industry Association!

What if I had never initiated that follow-up?

Most people struggle with follow-up for three reasons:

1. It feels like a huge time burden
2. Not knowing how to prioritize who they should follow-up with
3. Not knowing what to say or how to effectively handle a follow-up to make something meaningful and tangible happen

So let's break it down. I'll show you a new approach to follow-up as well as some super practical tips to becoming a master at follow-up and how you can produce some rip-roaring return on your follow-up investment.

Making Follow-Up A Priority — With Ease

I could tell you about how important follow-up is until the cows come home. Most likely you will agree with me wholeheartedly but do nothing or very little about it.

When you get back from a networking event, you've already invested time and energy. Now you have all these business cards and you have to do something with them. It seems overwhelming. When something seems overwhelming, we usually put it off or do nothing about it.

The solution is to break follow-up down into bite-sized steps.

Step 1. The First 30 Minutes Rule

When you put a networking event into your calendar, IMMEDIATELY block out the first half hour after the event to follow-up. This means that if you go to a breakfast meeting, put an extra half hour for follow-up into the calendar.

If you go to a lunch-time event, same thing. At night, if you get home at a reasonable hour, take 15–30 minutes for follow-up. Or block out the first half hour the following morning.

Step 2. Prioritize

You should follow-up with every person you took a business card from. That doesn't mean you have to meet with everyone.

I recommend 3 levels of follow-up and 3 priority categories.

Break your new connections into A, B, C levels of contacts.

A contacts are people you have an interest in, people who you think are smart, potential clients or relationships you'd like to develop, or people you think have outstanding networks.

B level contacts are somewhat interesting but you're not sure if you have all that much mutual opportunity, affinity or whether they have the kind of network you're interested in.

C contacts are limited in their appeal or opportunity but they're a possibility for the future.

For each level of contact you can choose one of 3 different levels of follow-up, each having a corresponding level of time investment.

Email — lowest level

Phone — second level

Face-to-face — highest level.

As you can see, the time investment for face-to-face is highest and should be reserved for A level connections, the highest potential relationships.

Also, in the lowest level, you can include invitations to connect on LinkedIn. It's easy, quick, and you can circle around to that person at a later date if you want to explore the relationship more fully.

One of the biggest mistakes people make is thinking they have to have lunch or breakfast with every person they meet at a networking event. If you have a phone meeting first and see that there could be more opportunity between you, great. Then you can take it to the next level.

On the other hand, you never know.

Let me tell you about Harvey.

I met Harvey at a networking group event. Harvey is a liability insurance agency owner. He looks the part too. You know what I mean — tall, lanky, conservative, not the most gregarious guy on the block.

So when I agreed to schlep over to meet Harvey, I was skeptical and annoyed with myself. I thought: I'm too busy to waste my time with this kind of person. (How arrogant I was!)

When Harvey and I sat down for coffee, and I started asking him about himself and his business, I was stunned.

Mr. Boring Insurance guy was a musician with 2 CD's to his credit, and he had a fabulous network of CEO's of top companies (he was on the board of several well-known non-profit organizations). The beauty of the non-profit connection is that top-level executives also sit on their boards. Harvey was interesting, highly connected, and super-generous. He immediately connected me with 3 referrals, and I hired him to handle all of my personal and business and insurance needs. Harvey was a hoot and we became fast friends.

Harvey had probably been on my C list of priorities. Fortunately, I took a chance. But if you notice, I had to dig a little to find the gold in Harvey, so make sure you explore a little to find out what category level a new contact actually belongs in.

Step 3. How To Follow-Up Brilliantly (And Get Everyone You Meet With To Say YES)

When I watched how challenged my clients were with follow-up, I literally created a tip sheet, a menu of sorts, to tell them things they could do to follow-up after the networking. If an immediate referral or opportunity didn't seem obvious, they didn't know what to say or do. The menu helped give them a roadmap of ideas to use to develop that relationship until a referral opportunity presented itself.

The point of follow-up is to build the relationship, not just to get an immediate referral.

The bigger point of follow-up, one that few people really talk about is to LEARN and LISTEN for opportunity.

Some of that opportunity will be for you directly.

But sometimes that opportunity is going to be for your colleagues and clients.

When you hear of an opportunity for your colleagues and clients, **your value shoots way up** because now you are an opportunity-provider not just an opportunity-seeker.

The Rule Of Three

If you want to ratchet up your networking productivity like lightning, use The Rule of Three.

For all your A preferred new contacts, make a plan to do 3 things for them to help their business. You can use The Rule of Three over time as long as you do 3 things within 3 months or less. That's the window that will have the greatest impact for your contact.

What's The Real Secret To Successful Follow-Up?

The key to follow-up is to make it a game and JUST DO IT! Look at it this way: if you've made the effort and investment in going to the networking event, and you do not follow-up, it's like turning on the ignition of your car but not stepping on the gas. If you don't step on the gas, you ain't getting anywhere. You will just be sitting in the same place with your motor running.

CHAPTER 14

How To Make Networking Your Personal Public Relations Engine

Some are born great, some achieve greatness,
and some hire public relations officers.
—Daniel J. Boorstin

A FEW YEARS AGO, I was hosting my first live event. I really wanted some good press coverage.

My dream coverage would be The Wall Street Journal and a few trade publications in law and accounting.

I asked a few of my favorite colleagues if they had any connections at those publications.

None of my connections had any connections to the press.

A big warning bell went off in my mind. My circle had no pull with the press! I realized this was a big gap that had to be filled.

As it turned out, my event did receive coverage by The Wall Street Journal, as well as three other trade publications. I did have to engage a PR agent, but at the same time, and more importantly, I also started cultivating relationships with people who had relationships with the press.

I went from having zero recognition to being featured in a regional business publication, quoted in The New York Times, The Daily News, on Fox Business News, and several trade publications.

Did this publicity get me new business?

That's the wrong question.

PR isn't a direct cause/effect link to new business.

It's designed to bring you visibility and credibility.

These are important additional factors when people are considering engaging you, but they don't necessarily cause new clients.

Are You Networked Into The Press?
Your Personal Brand Is At Stake

A few months ago, I was on Twitter and started having "tweet-versations" with a lawyer.

We eventually brought the "cloud to the ground" and had lunch.

I am always amazed at how you "never know" whom you are going to meet and what you will learn from their stories.

Tom (not his real name) is a prominent attorney in a big law firm.

He not only has a high-end practice but he also is a frequent on-air interviewee on CNN and a featured columnist in a leading business publication.

I asked him how he got his start as an on-air expert.

His story is very telling about strategically gaining the eyes and ears of the press.

Early in his career, Tom was building his practice. Coming from a family of politicians, he understood the importance of getting the right press and visibility.

Although Tom is naturally a savvy networker, he had not yet cultivated any connections in the press to enhance his visibility in the marketplace.

One day, he got a call from a local TV station asking for a quote on a story they were developing. As it turns out, the person who contacted

Tom was an assistant to the lead reporter on the story. Tom happily helped him out and told him to feel free to call on him to help him with any other stories he was hunting down.

This young assistant was eager to prove himself, a bit wet behind the ears, and Tom helped him get what he needed for the story, which made him look good with his boss.

A year or so later, Tom got a call from this assistant.

The assistant was now a lead reporter at a national network TV station. He was calling for a quote on a story he was reporting on. Would Tom be interested in giving his quote on camera?

The assistant was now a bigger cheese at a national network station, and Tom got national recognition and visibility. Thus, a bond was built between the press and Tom.

Tom is now a regular commentator on stations such as CNN and Fox Business News, and is a featured business columnist for Business Week.

The lesson here is to build your connections to the press at all levels. Eventually this will pay off with relationships that can help you gain immense credibility and visibility.

Not having any connections to writers or people in the press limits your ability to get bigger coverage and visibility.

However, today, we also have the benefit of using social media and do-it-yourself PR-enhancing online tools such as Help A Reporter Out (www.helpareporterout.com) and PR Leads (www.prleads.com) to help us connect to very effective public relations opportunities. These didn't exist just a few short years ago.

But what about building the buzz that comes from Word Of Mouth advertising? Can you leverage your network to up-level your "word of mouth" PR?

This is often called building your platform.

Word of Mouth publicity can be built by your social media connections — Facebook fans and Twitter followers, for example.

These people are your "tribe," your admirers. These are the people who like your fan page on FB, follow you on Twitter, tweet about you, connect and converse with you on LinkedIn, and post comments on your blog.

And they voluntarily forward your updates and say great things about you to their colleagues and friends.

Today, your network can be leveraged into your personal PR agency.

Common methods that you can employ to expand your platform by word of mouth:

1. **Ask for referrals and recommendations** — ask your most satisfied customers and clients if they know others who would like to have premium service or products such as yours. Ask your connections on LinkedIn to post official recommendations of you and your work.

2. **Ask for Likes** — invite all your colleagues, friends, LinkedIn contacts to "like" your facebook fan page (* a facebook fan page is your business page on Facebook as opposed to the page you put up for your personal posts and pictures)

3. **Invite comments on your blog.** If you are blogging, you will want to build and attract interaction and comments. Post your topics and posts to your email list, your Twitter followers, Facebook friends and fans, and LinkedIn connections. Invite their comments. This can be slow going until you build traction. Be patient and be consistent. Your traction will build. Getting featured on bigger bloggers' sites accelerates your visibility and fan club members.

4. **Build buzz through your own live events** — This is a great way to build your WOM visibility and fan status. Remember Gordon Einstein's story? You too can host simple events (happy hours), networking events, workshops

and seminars, CLE or CPE programs, or panel presentations and grow your credibility and visibility.

5. **Become a Connector** — This is my favorite approach. When you start to become known as introducing good people to other high-quality people, you will discover that these people generate a buzz about you —in a great way.

Building Your Network & Personal Brand For "POW"erful PR

You've probably heard or read about personal branding. What exactly is a personal brand and how does it differ from traditional product branding?

Years ago, branding meant primarily one thing: your company or product brand. We understood brand names immediately, such as Levis, Coca Cola, McDonalds and Nike. The Nike swoosh logo was enough to tell us what we would get if we bought a product with that swoosh on it.

As the world of marketing expanded into the service sector and the online marketing world, it was no longer just a product or company that was being branded.

Brand You was born.

For the first time, it wasn't just celebrities who were building a persona image and identity and transmitting it into the marketplace.

Now, every day, real people in the business community started to see that their "personal brand" would give them a huge edge up on the competition and allow them to catapult their business results. Social media only made that process cheaper, faster, and allowed one's personal brand to reach the four corners of the earth with a simple click.

Now too, one's personal brand could be used to sell services, not just tangible products.

You can become the brand. What you do is the product. Who you are can become the personal brand standing at the gateway to the product.

Building your personal brand can have a far-reaching impact not only in sales and marketing. It also allows you to attract a more select and desirable network of influencers. This network of influencers opens doors to opporunity that would have previously been inaccessible and unattainable.

Your Unique Personal Brand + Your Network Of Influencers = Extraordinary Opportunities

The power of the personal brand has been recognized by some of our most influential and successful thought leaders. While they had a role to fill, they could never have influenced as many or made their message known without cultivating their personal brand in their arena.

One of the best examples of someone who built a personal brand that rocked the world is Bill Clinton — Bill Clinton has a mixed bag going in his personal brand. His intent as President of the United States was to create policies and bring our country to a new level of prosperity at home and as a leader in the world.

But let's go deeper than just the label of President of The United States.

Intentionally, Bill built his personal brand around being deeply connected to people. He generated a warmth, caring, and accessibility as "one of us down-home folks" but smart enough to lead effectively.

On the flip side, his womanizing ways also became part of his personal brand, which diminished its strength.

But few have done a better job at using personal branding to make a difference with millions.

Another example is Tony Robbins — We associate Tony with motivation and success, don't we? If you want success in life, he's the go-to guru. We know he pioneered life coaching and turned it into a marketable brand. Some of the world's biggest talents have called upon Tony to coach them out of life and career slumps into new realms of success, from Andre Agassi to Mark Burnett, Executive Producer of the show, Survivor, to Marc Benioff, CEO of Salesforce.com.

Oprah — Oprah did a brilliant thing. After years as a successful daytime TV talk show host, she transformed her already huge personal brand into spiritual leader, helping others achieve their best life ever, and connecting on a heart-based level with her viewers. That's when her influence really skyrocketed into the stratosphere.

But what if you're not a celebrity? Few of us are, and fewer of us want to be.

Does this mean everyone can have a recognizable marketable brand?

Not only is my answer a resounding YES! but I say it is essential that you "brand yourself like a fox".

Your personal brand will empower you further in your Networking Up.

Targeted networking and building a powerful personal brand are linked like peanut butter and jelly.

How To Build Your Personal Brand To
Attract Your Perfect Niche Market

It always comes back to two things:

Knowing who you are and what you stand for — authentically
Knowing exactly who your ideal audience is — your niche.

What I mean by this is if you don't resonate with corporate types of people, but are more free-wheeling, and artistic or creative, it will take something to build a personal brand that resonates with and attracts the corporate community.

If you are more artistic and creative, your audience will be the creatives; they will resonate with you and you with them.

Therefore, you have to be very clear (and I mean crystal clear) about your niche market.

The better you zero in on the right market — this could be the industry, the position, the geographical location, the demographics, the gender, the circumstances, marital status, family status — the better you will understand their problems and needs.

Harrison has a recruiting/staffing business. His niche: electrical engineering executives.

Harrison had to have the right personal brand — trustworthy, humble — to appeal to the technical types in the electrical engineering world.

You need to think about how you want your niche market to see you, think of you, talk about you.

Personal branding doesn't happen overnight.

When it comes to building your personal brand, everything counts:

The way you dress, walk, communicate, ask questions, your voice, where you hang out, who you hang out with.

It all goes into the cake mix when baking your personal brand.

This discussion is bringing me back to when I began building my own personal brand. Up until I left my corporate career, my personal brand was corporate executive. But when I left that world, I was brandless. It felt pretty strange to not have that personal "corporate executive" brand and identity to stand behind.

That's when I realized I needed to create a new personal brand. I found my personal brand quite by accident — it actually came from one of my favorite books —one I've mentioned before — *The Tipping Point* by Malcolm Gladwell.

I read that book and was totally blown away by reading about one of the three kinds of business people that create tipping point results — The Connector. I thought if only I could find my Connector, I'd be able to meet and attract all the clients I could want.

I spent a year and a half looking for my Connector — a connector, according to Gladwell, is a highly connected person with lots of powerful relationships who can connect you to many influential relationships. Fortunately, I never found my Connector because it inspired me to actually become a Connector myself. And that's how I built my personal brand as someone who can be counted on to introduce and connect business people with valuable new relationships.

This allowed me to build a really large and successful network, certainly helped me attract the kinds of clients I would never have been able to had I not built this personal brand, and it made a big difference for all the people I was able to connect in my community. It was fun, fruitful and helped me build an influential personal brand.

But the most remarkable personal brand I ever saw created was by my former company colleague Marty.

Marty was at one time your basic CFO in a major corporation. His personal brand was completely non-descript — another smart finance guy in a navy blue suit.

But fortunately, Marty was fired. He left his corporate career behind him and started his own wealth management and financial advisory business.

Marty was definitely a smart financial professional. However, he knew — because there was so much competition in the wealth management arena — that he would have to create a memorable, influential personal brand quickly. Smart wasn't good enough.

Here's the picture: Marty starts his business in an affluent community — one that is pretty traditional and conservative.

The first time I went to see Marty after his departure from Corporate America was the biggest lesson in personal branding I ever got.

I was expecting the old Marty in his corporate navy-blue suit uniform.

Well....

In walks Marty — completely shaved head, full beard, an earring in one ear, white button down shirt, blue jeans, white sneakers — and the piece de resistance — a bow tie.

Crazy? Crazy like a fox.

Marty built a multi-million dollar investment firm in the space of just under 7 years in a very tough economy.

His secret? He certainly was brilliant at finance. He knew how to help people's money work for them.

But that's what all the other wealth advisors did.

What Marty did was build a personal brand built on mystique. People thought he was quirky but also mysterious, unusual. His personal brand helped people believe that he had secrets to wealth the other guys didn't.

It worked.

Marty built a wealth management empire including celebrities, captains of industry, and centers of influence based on his financial smarts and **enhanced by** his distinctive personal brand.

How To Leverage Your Network To Spread Your Brand
When you are working on up-leveling your network, seeking to attract and build relationships with high-quality decision makers, influencers, and mentors, your personal brand will be a launch pad for new connections as much as, maybe even more than your business card.

Rob Levin is a man who sought out a top notch mentor and got one because of this strategy.

Read how this helped him build a fantastic personal brand and a super successful publication business.

CASE STUDY
Rob Levin
CEO & Publisher
The New York Enterprise Report

Rob Levin has a lot of letters after his name letting us know he's a well educated, smart, business savvy guy: CPA, MBA, CFO, CEO. But after years in accounting and business leadership roles, he still didn't know a thing about publishing a magazine or working for himself. But that's what he really wanted to do.

While working at another media company as a short-term CEO, he met Rose Sullivan, a magazine publishing expert. Rob was not shy about reaching out to strangers. While they didn't work together at that time, he kept in touch with Rose and when he came up with the idea for a magazine catering to NY's small business community he made a quick call to Rose that helped Rob learn a lot about the costs, printing, and logistics of producing a magazine.

In 2003, after reading an article by Norm Brodsky, the highly successful entrepreneur and well-known columnist for INC Magazine, Rob reached out and asked Norm for a meeting. He went to visit him in Brooklyn asking for feedback on his business plan for The New York Enterprise Report. The business model, among other things, entailed paid subscriptions.

Although Norm would not tell Rob what he thought about the business idea, he did go through the plan with Rob in detail. After drilling through the numbers and assumptions, he asked Rob why not consider giving the magazine away for FREE!

Rob, stunned, initially balked at the idea. He knew there was going to be such great value in the magazine. Why give this away for nothing?

After a restless night of sleep, Rob saw the wisdom in Norm's idea, and decided to build a controlled subscriber base (free to qualified readers). It worked! Norm Brodsky was the first cover feature on The New York Enterprise Report. Their relationship of mentor and protoge turned into real friendship, and ultimately Norm invested in the company.

A year after Rob launched the magazine, Norm 'fessed up and told Rob he hadn't really wanted to meet with Rob and that he thought his idea for the magazine was "dumb." Well, even Norm isn't right 100% of the time. But Rob feels meeting Norm and taking his input was a key ingredient for the magazine's success. Today, The New York Enterprise Report is a thriving media company.

Rob has turned his acquired knowledge of networking with the right people into a successful business model as well. The New York Enterprise Report now brings together hundreds of entrepreneurs to network with other like-minded entrepreneurs at highly acclaimed events and seminars (including the Small Business Awards).

When Rob started out in his career, he admits he didn't establish relationships or maintain them successfully. Recognizing his networking and business development skills were lacking, he took training to improve.

Rob says it is easy to be impressed by people initially. So he is careful with whom he develops relationships. (I can vouch for this. It took years for me to gain Rob's attention and trust) He is strategic about whom he is introduced to and to whom he introduces others. He carefully considers whether value can be brought to both parties.

> In Rob's view, social capital and influence is developed when you can have value for people who are influential themselves.

People will get a sense of your personal brand within the first 15–20 seconds of meeting you.

That's why I heartily recommend that people work on their appearance, voice, handshake, smile, ability to ask smart questions, eye contact, body language, and listening skills.

The best appearance and handshake in the world won't help you if you can't stop running off at the mouth and turning people off.

I can't even count the times I observe Diarrhea Of The Mouth Syndrome.

How To Construct Your Powerful Personal Brand

Your personal brand is created on three fronts:

1. Your image and physical presence
2. Your value proposition —what you do and how you do it in a way that is unique and needed by your target market
3. Your message — what you say, how you say it, how you listen to others

All three contribute to being able to leverage your personal brand into a top-drawer network.

A few quick tips to bolster your personal brand:

1. **Dress in alignment with your audience, but add one unusual and memorable element.** For women, it could be your glasses that are memorable; for men, you might always wear a red tie. For the 20-somethings techie community,

casual is chic. One of my colleagues in the cool techie community always wears a dark grey t-shirt — it's his personal brand. (Remember Marty? His personal brand was a bow tie and an aura of mystery)

2. **Confidence builds connection.** Fake it until you make it. This is the only time I ever recommend being fake about anything. No one wants to hang out with someone who is unsure of themselves and spreads that around. The secret here is this: everyone experiences a lack of confidence sometimes. Even the biggest CEO's don't like walking into a room full of strangers. Fake confidence until you feel it; it will start to build once you meet the right people.

3. **Ask better probing questions; then really listen.** When people realize that you are interested in them, you become immensely interesting. This begins to build your personal brand with them. It elevates you in their eyes. They become attracted to and interested in you. Then your relationship can start to develop.

4. **Expect very little; give a lot.** Don't expect tit for tat. Think about whom you can connect with or refer to these decision makers. Are you already doing this? Great! Do more of it, and be more creative with it. Mention them in your blog, help them promote a speaking gig they are leading, introduce them to good people.

Now that your personal brand is baking and is about to come out of the oven, you want that wonderful aroma to spread and you want others to wonder where that great aroma is coming from.

Here are 9 Ways to leverage/spread your personal brand to your ideal network without buying ads or using a press release:

1. Use it as a tag line on your business card
2. Use it to attract and land speaking gigs
3. Use it as the signature on your email
4. Use it in your bio/excerpt when you write an article or blogpost
5. Use it in your video captions
6. Use it to get featured/quoted by the press
7. Use it in your networking group and online social network bios
8. Use it on your website bio
9. Use it in your 30-second elevator pitch

By leveraging your personal brand, you will attract your ideal colleagues, prospective clients, and referrers.

By sharing your personal brand continuously and consistently, people will be spreading the word for you.

Take notice of who starts to reach out to you after you begin using this strategy and watch the new level of contacts and how your network is growing.

CHAPTER 15

Your 30-Second Elevator Pitch: Pitch Like A Fox

I think that while markets are conversations, marketing is a story.
—Seth Godin

WHAT HAPPENS WHEN you finally do meet your "sweet spot" influencers and decision makers? What do you say when they ask you, "So what do you do?"

The image of being face-to-face with influencers and decision makers often terrifies even the most experienced networker.

This is truly where the rubber meets the road.

People often size us up within the first 3–7 seconds of meeting us. That's why so many articles and blog posts and books focus on how to design and deliver the ideal 30-second elevator pitch. As you can see by the numbers, 30-seconds is often too long. We really need to captivate someone in just a few seconds.

I'm going to dive in and teach you how to "pitch like a fox" so that you are memorable, engaging, and create the beginnings of rewarding relationships with even the most illustrious people.

The 30-Second Elevator Pitch: A Necessity And A Curse

I'm discussing the elevator pitch because in reality, you need to have one. But while it's needed, it is also a curse and a detriment.

So why bother delving into it, especially when it's so difficult to create a great one?

First, let's look at why they don't work.

The Elevator Pitch, that quick sound bite where you try to tell the world what you do and why it's something they want to hear about, is overused, over-massaged, contrived.

The more we try to make it memorable and cute, the worse and the more inauthentic we sound.

I know the elevator pitch isn't going away anytime soon; in fact, I've blogged about ways to make it memorable and even irresistible.

However, what if you took a different approach?

When you meet someone, the very first thing they expect to know is 'what do you do?' It's a way for people to get a sense of you and why they will want to connect with you.

A new approach is to give a tag line about what you do.

One lawyer expressed this tag line, "I win business cases."

An accountant said, "I'm an IRS shield"

One of my colleagues who is a membership director for a networking organization called herself "a professional networker."

Said with a bit of humor, it can really be a great icebreaker and make a new connection fun and interesting.

Creating a tag line makes what you do short and memorable and even fun.

But we don't just want to leave people hanging with a sound bite.

We can layer the sound bite with something meaty and tangible.

That's why I've been recommending people shift from "elevator pitch formula" into what I call the "tanecdote" method.

How A Tanecdote Works

A tanecdote is a blend of your tag line plus a short example of how you did something successful for a client, an anecdote, if you will.

A tanectdote might sound like:

I'm a client attraction trainer for lawyers.

An example is I showed a client how to niche their practice and build a multi-six figure law practice in traffic law from scratch

Or

People call me a social media megaphone. Using social media techniques, I helped my t-shirt manufacturing client get more visible, which ultimately led to a spot on the Good Morning America show.

Or

People call my firm the social media megaphone. We helped a consultant client get 3 clients through their connections on LinkedIn.

Crafting a tanecdote takes as much thought and strategy as an elevator pitch. The advantage is it transforms the typical "what do you do?" answer into a fresh way of sharing how you have **produced tangible results** through your endeavors.

This is a new approach that will make people sit up and take notice in a good way.

In the Network Like A Fox Action Guide, I'll be walking you through this process and giving you some punchy and specific ways to craft a tag line and select an anecdote that can engage and even entertain.

Remember, the objective is to have your new contact say, "Really, that's interesting, tell me more."

CHAPTER 16

Choosing Your Significant Other/ Life Partner Can Make Or Break Your Network & Business

A man's wife can either make him or break him,
but the reasons why aren't always clear.
—Napoleon Hill

WHEN NAPOLEON HILL wrote these words back in 1937, most men worked, women stayed home and cared for the house and family.

Today, he probably would have revised this statement to say:

A person's significant other or life partner can either make or break him/her, but the reasons aren't always clear.

As I began writing this book, and conducting the interviews with the successful people whose case studies I've been sharing with you, I began to notice a trend:

Quite a number of them were telling me how they met certain key influencers or connected with certain opportunities through their significant other or life partner/spouse.

This led me to thinking:

Beyond the personal happiness received through romantic love and the relationship,

"Does the choice of your significant other impact who you meet and thus impact your level of success in business and life?"

Sandra was a young, rising star in the commercial real estate business. She was hard working, smart, and was making progress — slowly. Her biggest challenge was finding and landing the big listings. She just didn't know enough of the right people.

Her last marriage had ended in a sad divorce but Sally was still optimistic. On Thursday nights, she sang in a church choir. Singing was a passion. Music was a passion. Real Estate paid the bills.

One night, a guest pianist accompanied the choir. He was a friend of the choir conductor. Sandra sang a solo and caught the attention and the heart of the pianist.

That chance meeting led not only to a rousing romance but to a whole new world for Sandra.

Coincidentally, the pianist had rejected his family business in favor of his true love — music. He came from a very prominent family in real estate — a household name real estate family.

Sandra didn't know this when she met him. They just clicked! But as their relationship blossomed and led to marriage, Sandra became exposed to the elite in the real estate world. Family events, dinners, holidays and outings included many of the movers and shakers in the real estate world.

Her father-in-law was not only a family member; he also became her mentor and taught her many of the secrets of the real estate world in a curriculum it would have taken her decades to acquire on her own. She gained savvy and a network that catapulted her career.

While her husband had no interest in real estate, Sandra was a sponge for everything she could learn and leverage.

It was a stroke of fortune that led Sandra to love and to a powerful professional universe all in one fell swoop.

Sandra didn't actively seek out a romance with someone who had the right connections in real estate. It just happened.

But it gets you to wondering….

How important is it to find the right life partner if you want to be connected to the right people?

I found the research for the writing of this chapter illuminating and inspiring.

Why? Because I cannot think of a single book on networking that addresses this issue dead on. It's like it's a taboo subject. Nothing could be a bigger omission from the conversation about connecting successfully than not talking about whom you are dating or building your life with. It's vitally important!

You've heard the old adage: It's just as easy to love a rich man (or woman) as a poor one.

Ok, that's a little crass and smacks of advising you to marry or choose your lover based on his or her wealth or connections.

It's an age-old strategy and many still do this.

That is not what this exploration is about. Networking like a fox does not mean you should mate for money.

The Person With Whom You Mate Determines Which Big Cheeses You Meet

It is an absolute fact: your choice of a life partner will affect the level and kind of success you have in business and career.

Let me give you a few examples.

I'm going to take you behind the curtain of my life a bit here.

My ex-husband David was, at one time, my boss.

That's right, I married the boss.

He was so smart and insanely funny. How could I resist that?

Well, there were some big benefits to this relationship that even my blinded-by-love eyes couldn't see.

As it turned out, shortly after we married, David decided to change careers and go into business in the financial services industry. I decided to stay in women's underwear (no snickers, please).

The company where we met eventually went through an IPO and we both got very attractive golden parachute packages. I took a job with a bigger company in the industry. David became a professional financial advisor.

But even though I was now ready to be promoted from middle management to a VP level, if you have ever worked inside a company or corporation, you know it is generally harder to get promoted from within than by jumping to another company to get to the next level.

One of David's best friends, Richard, had been my boss at a previous employer of mine. He was now President of the U.S. division of a Japanese company. It was a high-end, highly prestigious company.

I heard that Richard's company had recently lost their VP of Marketing to another competitor and that slot was open. I wanted it and I wanted it badly.

I had applied for that job a couple of years earlier, before I was married to David, but had been passed over.

Now here's where it gets interesting — I got a firsthand look at how big cheeses curry favor with other big cheeses.

First, I had to transition my image in Richard's mind from family friend to serious contender. I told David I wanted to apply and asked him to help me get the job.

Anyone who has worked with a spouse knows it is not always easy to take coaching from a spouse.

But David coached me on how to apply properly for this role and how to handle myself in the interview.

Richard was a tough interviewer and even though he was now a friend of mine, I had my work cut out for me to earn this job.

David's coaching and endorsement to Richard really made a difference.

But here's where having the right partner also helped immensely.

When you are up-leveling your career, one of the biggest stumbling blocks is in negotiating for your up-leveled salary (or fee if you are in your own business).

David and I spent hours practicing my pitch to Richard on what I wanted for my salary package.

Since David was a "big boy" who had negotiated high level packages with some very big executives, he helped me navigate these tricky waters.

To Richard, I was no longer just a candidate; I was a known, trusted contender. I was vetted. Richard now knew me, and he saw me as someone who had the right experience as well as someone who would have his back and could be an asset to him and his company

The most important thing I learned in this process is determining leverage — how much each person has and how to use it.

I got the job!

Using the techniques David and I had mapped out, I literally doubled my income in one fell swoop and achieved my first VP title before the age of 40. That had been my goal! I was ecstatic, and it was the big career break I needed.

Selecting David as my partner made a very big difference to my network. As a senior executive he knew a lot of other senior executives. He was respected, and by osmosis, I was respected.

He was also a willing mentor and coach. Had he not been supportive or willing, that would have altered my entire career path.

Your mate can be a source of love and fulfillment; he or she can also be a door opener to whole new worlds for you.

Now, I'd like to introduce you to Pablo Solomon, a very talented artist. His story is a powerful picture of how your life partner can connect you with real success.

CASE STUDY
Pablo Solomon
World Renowned Artist
Your Mate Can Hold Your Heart And The
Link To Your Success

Pablo Solomon is a talented artist.

But for decades, he was living the common sad saga of the struggling artist: boundless vision, talent, and drive but still undiscovered and unable to make a living doing what he loved to do most.

His work, mostly drawings and sculptures of dancers, as well as environmentally-oriented designs, sat widely unnoticed and largely unsold.

Fortunately, Pablo was married to Beverly. Beverly was not only an emotionally supportive wife, but she also held an important key to the turning point in Pablo's career.

Pablo's wife Beverly was, in her earlier years, a successful model, and then later a marketing executive in some prestigious companies — Diane von Furstenburg, Revlon, and Ralph Lauren.

But Beverly, keenly aware of and committed to helping Pablo, wisely realized that she had an untapped resource: her old network of influencers.

One day, Beverly called one of her successful and well-connected friends, Marilyn, whom she had met working at a French cosmetics company. Beverly told Marilyn about Pablo's talent and long-time struggle, and asked for her help. Marilyn agreed with the proviso that if she saw in Pablo's work what Beverly saw, and he agreed, Pablo would have to follow her coaching to the letter. Pablo gave a big YES to this challenge.

Marilyn immediately saw the potential in Pablo's artwork. But she also saw that he was rough around the edges and needed a major make-over — both in rebranding his style and in how his work was presented.

Pablo let his mentor remake and transform him. Then, and only then, when he was ready for a debut with his mentor's art world movers and shakers, did Marilyn present Pablo and his work to a major art collector. This was the turning point in Pablo's career.

Today, Pablo Solomon is an internationally recognized artist and designer, whose work has been featured in museums all over the world. He has been featured in 23 books, numerous major magazines and newspapers, radio, TV and film.

Having come from "rags" to recognition, Pablo has gleaned some great aha's about networking. In a telling interview, he shared some powerful nuggets with me:

Pablo, in his earlier years, met some wealthy collectors through a friend. But at the time, not being cognizant of how important it is to make the right "influencer" connections, he missed out on some promising opportunities.

Pablo says to people who want to build relationships with "just the right people": "The challenge is just as much staying away from the "wrong" people as meeting the right people. Sorting out the good from the bad, and choosing your friends wisely will lead to good opportunities. If you don't dump the negative people in your life, it will certainly lead to negative results."

One of Pablo's best tips: "Keep a journal and contact list of everyone you meet. I lost touch with so many wonderful, talented and creative people over the years. I also lost track of people with fabulous connections. I was fortunate to have selected not only a very supportive wife, but one who had the vision and the connections to help me learn and leverage my talent with the right people."

I love Pablo and Beverly's story because it shows that connecting wisely in your personal life is important for your confidence and professional growth, and most certainly for the connections leading to greater success.

Currently Pablo lives and works with his wife Beverly on their historic 1856 ranch north of Austin, Texas.

Your Mate Determines The Emotional And Psychic Support You Get

In my case, David and I eventually divorced (the financial services business took its toll on him and our relationship) but his guidance and connecting me in my career will be forever appreciated.

A spouse or life partner can be the biggest confidence builder or psychic vampire in one's world. The success of your business or career can be monumentally influenced by how strongly your spouse or partner encourages or dissuades you.

Think and Grow Rich, by Napoleon Hill is one of the iconic business books of the 20th century and still remarkably timely and relevant to this day. Napoleon talks about staying away from doing business with friends and family if you want to be exceptionally successful.

Why? Because friends, family, and especially life partners, are often fearful of your possible failure and how it will affect the family finances and routine.

They can see your dreams as a financial drain rather than an opportunity.

They can see your dream as a distraction so they receive less of your time and attention.

They can see your dream as a threat to the status quo and the current order of family life.

They can see your dream as a danger to a dependable monthly income.

OR, on the other hand…

They can see your dream as an opportunity to build a bigger, better life.

They can see themselves as a support to your vision and as a way to build something bigger and better together.

Who you are in relationship with is who you are

Make no mistake about it:

Supportive partner = greater success.

Fearful, angry, doubtful partner = doubtful success.

A partner who is angry or resentful about your taking a chance on a business venture or always talking about why something won't work will drain your energy, confidence, and performance.

A supportive partner will boost your spirits and your self-confidence when things don't go right, when you hit speed bumps, when you want to throw in the towel, and when you need ideas.

Pick your partner wisely. Your career and business depend on it.

It really saddens me to see people fearful of their partners. Often, they will tell me things like, "I cannot make a decision on my own that affects my partner." Of course, this is what partnership is all about. But more often they are saying this because they fear getting major push-back from a spouse or significant other and don't feel they have the wherewithal to convince or enroll their partner to support them in making an investment in time, effort and money to go after their dreams and goals.

I am a huge believer in getting input from one's partner. But isn't partnership supposed to be supporting each other's personal development as well as the couple's?

It is a slippery slope when you kill off someone's dream to protect your own feeling of safety.

I've been there and know how terrible it feels to not be able to live and be oneself fully because a partner is jealous, fearful or angry.

Change is scary to all around you and you need to be sensitive to that.

You also deserve to honor your desire to live full out, play bigger, and thrive. It is for you and your family, not just for yourself.

Sometimes it is hard for those around you to appreciate this. Sometimes, in time, they get it. Sometimes they don't. It is never living authentically if you are in fear or worried about what your spouse or partner will think if you go after your dream.

That is why choosing a partner who has the desire and ability to endorse you living fully in this world can make or break your career. This choice cuts both ways because both partners have to feel fulfilled and supported by each other.

To network like a fox it is ideal to mate like a fox as well.

Picking A Mate With Knowledge And Skills
From Which You Can Learn And Grow

If you hang around with smart people, you will learn more.

If you hang around with not-so-smart or not-so-motivated people, your life will be more limited.

That's why your parents always told you to hang out with the smart, good kids.

When it comes to career and business, there are some remarkable advantages to mating with a smart person or someone with special talents and skills.

Karen was married to a man who was a financial advisor, a very successful money manager. He not only had friends in high financial places, but he also showed her the inner workings of the investment world, the world that lay investors never see. Karen learned how to invest money wisely and leveraged this knowledge when, after getting her license, she formed her own advisory firm for women.

Angela Kim has a successful spa in NYC. She is also the renowned founder of Savor The Success, an online community for women entrepreneurs, especially product/brick and mortar-based entrepreneurs.

When Angela launched Savor The Success, she needed a special web-based platform. Building custom web sites and platforms is very expensive. It's also challenging to find the right service providers.

Angela was fortunate to have selected the right mate. Her husband is a techy web-developer. The Savor site was a team vision and built by her hubby. Had Angela gone out and hired this talent she likely would still have been successful (after all her idea is outstanding) but it might have taken much longer and cost much more money to accomplish this success.

Savor The Success became a great success and having a committed, supportive mate with the right knowledge and skill greased the wheels to success.

My marriage to David taught me many things. You may laugh at this but one of the most important things I learned because of my relationship to David was how to work with computers.

David was an early adopter of the personal computer.

I was a slow learner but he drummed into me that the future was in computers and he was right.

He taught me how to use Word and many other applications for home computing.

Eventually he taught me about logging on to the World Wide Web when it was really brand new.

Left to my own devices, it would have taken me years to get into the world of online possibilities.

Because David was so smart and such an advanced thinker, it rubbed off on me. I believe it's one of the reasons I've been bitten by the techy bug and am not afraid of using technology for my business.

When Barry Met Sally In Sales

Barry met Sally at work. He was in marketing; she was in sales. Barry's father happened to be head of the Sales Department, which is how they met. When Sally and Barry married, Barry's father, now Sally's father-in-law, gave her the inside scoop about the sales process, getting connected to the buyers, closing deals, and even how to be more successful in the company.

Barry and Sally loved each other, but it was a pure bonus that Barry's father was able to help Sally ramp up her business and sales skills through his excellent mentorship.

Who Your Mate Is Is Who You Are

You are who you're married to. We've all heard it many times. Your world will revolve around your partner's world.

Emma (not her real name) was in a relationship with a man, Stuart, who was in recovery for alcoholism. He had been sober and in recovery for a very long time. As part of his recovery, he gave back to others in recovery.

Most of Stuart's social circle was comprised of people in recovery.

He was a powerful, smart, charismatic guy who gave back to his recovery community.

As a result Emma and Stuart's social circle was heavily slanted to interacting with people in recovery. A few had moved beyond the early stages of recovery and were successful in business and life.

Many in their circle were still grappling with getting their lives and careers back on track, and were grateful to have stable jobs. Rightfully, many were focused on getting healthy vs. getting ahead.

This had a great impact on Emma and her own business progress.

She played a whole lot smaller for fear of looking too materialistic, too self-focused.

She wasn't really aware of it because she loved Stuart. Emma admired him and appreciated his struggles and goals. But they weren't hers, and she made Stuart's goals hers instead of being herself and living into a bigger vision for her life.

Ultimately, Emma had to choose: be who she was or live Stuart's life.

Stuart really wasn't able or willing to support Emma in playing a bigger game so ultimately Emma chose to be herself and live into her potential.

As soon as Emma and Stuart parted, Emma's business took off in ways she could never have imagined.

More importantly, while she missed Stuart, Emma no longer felt like a stranger in her own skin. A giant weight had been lifted off her shoulders. She was able to thrive, grow, and give more of herself to others.

She was now able to live life on purpose.

CASE STUDY
Mary Buffett:
Best-selling Author & World Renowned Speaker

A number of years ago, I had the privilege of meeting a very special woman at a networking event for professionals.

She was doing a reading from her newest best-selling book on investing. I was immediately drawn in by her memorable voice and the very direct and powerful information she was sharing.

After the reading, I went up to the author to tell her how much I enjoyed her writing. Over the years, we stayed in touch and became friends and colleagues.

I watched as my friend Mary released many more best-selling books.

Mary began her notable career in the music publishing business. Growing up in Los Angeles, her sister was her first connector, introducing her to a revolving door of music industry innovators. Mary had an awesome voice — perfect pitch to be exact.

But in 1981, her fortune changed dramatically — personally and professionally — when she met and fell in love with a talented musician named Peter.

Mary's passion for Peter started with music. But what followed was completely unexpected — and demonstrates the remarkable ripple effect of one's choice of life partner.

It so happened that Peter's family, from Omaha, Nebraska, was headed by a brilliant financial investment icon.... Warren Buffett. Suddenly, the newly married Mary not only found herself a member of one of the wealthiest families in America, but also directly exposed to the teachings and investment philosophies of the most successful investor in America.

Mary's life was forever changed by her marriage to Peter Buffett and her exposure to Warren Buffett.

She now was learning all about personal finance and investing at the knee of the best and brightest investor of our time.

Sitting around the Christmas dinner table and other family functions, Mary met and listened to conversations with all sorts of captains of industry and thought leaders.

For the 12 years that Mary was married to Peter Buffett, a whole new world of learning, growth and connections opened up that would have been impossible otherwise.

Mary did not marry Peter Buffett for his money; she married for love.

Yet who she was "hanging around" with as a result of this relationship changed her life forever — even after her divorce from Peter and she was no longer present at Buffett family functions.

Mary's big WHY and purpose became a commitment to teaching and inspiring others about personal finances and investing by applying Warren's investing principles.

Today, she is not only a best-selling author many times over (Buffetology, The Tao Of Warren Buffett) but a world-wide speaker sharing the stage with icons such as Gen. Colin Powell, Rudy Guliani, Terry Bradshaw, Bill Cosby, and Laura Bush, sharing what she's learned from her ex-father-in-law with thousands of people all over the world.

Mary's story is a real nugget of gold because it demonstrates clearly that who you bond yourself with has enormous impact, on many levels, on what you fill your mind with, who you meet, what opportunities open up to you, and most important of all, the kind of contribution you can make back to the world.

When Your Mate Becomes Your Partner In Business

Sometimes, your life partner also becomes your partner in business.

It is miraculous when two people find their soul mate and their business mate all rolled into one.

But make no mistake: miracles are not always easy to live with. This path is often fraught with obstacles and bumps in the road.

How do you keep the problems of the business from infecting the love in the relationship?

How do you help the relationship thrive when you are busy building a business?

How do you manage the power struggles in the business without destroying the love and the balance of power and influence in the personal time of the relationship?

What happens to the business when the relationship changes or withers?

Working with your love partner is a huge decision. It can be exhilarating or exhausting. Often it is both.

Alan and Dianne Collins formed QuantumThink21 in the 1990's

Dianne is the creative force in the relationship.

Alan is the marketing/business component in the relationship.

Dianne creates the programs.

Alan sells and delivers them.

They have very different personalities. Dianne is a no-holds barred, tell-it-like-it-is type. Alan is a master mentor with super fine coaching and sales skills.

When I asked them how they made their relationship and the business work, Alan replied:

"We are committed to making a difference with people and providing transformation that is bigger than our relationship."

"When the relationship experiences challenges and disagreements we always come back to our purpose, one that is bigger than simply Alan and Dianne as a couple."

They have been married and working together for two decades.

Other couples have found that they have excellent complimentary skills and talents, but not the ability to keep relationship and business separate, or separate the power issues of the relationship from spilling over into the business.

The Bottom Line About Your Mate And Your Business Life

So what do you do when your wife, husband, girlfriend, boyfriend, or significant other can't or won't support you, diminishes you, and doesn't have the tools or willingness to be an asset to helping you build a bigger and better network and have a professional life that fulfills you?

Many clients have asked me whether they should stay or leave a relationship that drains them.

I would never be so presumptuous as to advise people on the advisability of whether they should stay or break from a life partner.

The biggest relationship storms start by an unintended misstep. Your mate begins to feel the business or the new people you are meeting are more important than the relationship.

Or you feel resentful because your partner can't or won't help you or support your going after your dream.

Talking this through and finding creative ways to include your partner and ask for support are essential for a thriving supportive personal relationship.

The right partner can be a boost to revving up your networking success or rob you of it. This is a reminder that you have a great deal of power in helping your partner help you be a peak performer. Win-win-win.

Get professional help when you sense things going off-track.

It's easier and more cost effective to take some preventative medicine than letting a problem develop into a full-blown illness.

At the end of the day, for true success to be attained, each person in the relationship must be to be true to who they really are and honest with one another.

CHAPTER 17

Become A Connector:
Rev Up Your Attraction Factor

NINE TIMES OUT OF TEN, people will read a book like this to improve networking results (a good idea) and skill at developing relationships with the right people (an even better idea).

Only a few are really concerned with how to connect others to one another so that *they are successful* in business. Yet, this is the smartest idea of all.

Connectors and Introducers, the people who bring people from various circles together, thereby helping everyone they connect expand their success, are people most in demand and appealing to others.

Who doesn't want to hang around people who are trying to help you?

The beauty of becoming a Connector is it takes all of the pressure of trying to "get" something off your shoulders. Once you're focused on helping others, you're a magnet for opportunity without any effort.

Here's how you becoming a Connector helps your connectees:
1. It makes it easier for them to meet the right people for their business.
2. It helps them build their visibility in a crowded marketplace.
3. It gives them access to more opportunities.

Here's how becoming a Connector helps you:
1. You're seen as a giver/contributor vs. a taker.
2. You build your self-confidence.
3. You grow a fabulous network faster and receive more opportunities for your business.
4. You gain rapid credibility and build a desirable personal brand fast.

Happily, once honed, Connector skills are transferrable, portable.

When I moved to California, I was able to transfer my connecting skills to new contacts. It took me a while to figure out where to network, gather a list of quality contacts and start introducing them to each other. But right from the get-go, I began to seek out not only people whom I thought would be good for my business, but people whom I thought others would like to meet.

One of my recent goals was to be invited to become a member of a particular professionals group in Los Angeles, one where I would develop a strong bond with the other professional members in my niche network (mostly boutique lawyers, accountants, and skilled professionals).

Doing my networking research, I found the right organization that focused on trusted advisors and professionals. It had about 2000 members in hundreds of chapter groups throughout California. Before choosing my main chapter group, I could try out several groups before making a final selection.

The group at the top of my list had a wonderful leader. When I asked her about joining her group, she was very nice but said her group was only taking on non-consultant members. They had already reached their quota of non-lawyer members.

I understood this. It was very smart leadership to be carefully creating the right mix of expertise in the group. While I was disappointed, I respected her decision.

I went my merry way, networking as usual. Soon, I met someone whom I thought would be a great referral source for this leader and connected them.

Then, knowing she was looking for additional lawyers for her group, I connected her with a lawyer who was looking for a new networking opportunity. I thought they'd be a great fit because this lawyer specialized in an area not already covered in the leader's group.

A couple of days later, I received a voice mail message from the leader. She had met with the group's Executive Committee and she brought my name up. They were inviting me to visit the group, making an exception to invite me to join because they saw my willingness to connect people and support the group even though I wasn't a member.

I was stunned and pleased. It really thrilled me to see how just doing what I love to do naturally, to connect people, turned into something so rewarding.

I didn't connect people to her to "get" something. I just thought she was the right person to be introduced to my colleagues.

But I never would have received the invitation had I not become a Connector.

Very soon after moving to California, I met other Connectors and we started cross connecting. It became a fantastic game and definitely helped me expand my personal brand and my business in Los Angeles.

Sometimes you meet someone exceptional, someone highly connected, and you just don't have an ideal referral for them. And you think " This person knows everyone, I don't have anything or anyone for this person so I can't be of value to him/her."

This reminds me of a great story I heard awhile back:

Donald Trump (let's not focus on his bad hair for a moment) is easily one of the wealthiest and most connected people in the world.

During one of the well-publicized times The Donald was going through a financial downturn, he was having a difficult time getting financing for one of his real estate projects.

One evening, although he was in no mood to mingle, he arrived at a fund raiser he had promised to attend.

As he was being seated at his table for dinner, he turned to a gentleman sitting next to him. He didn't know his dinner companion, but his table-mate was certainly acquainted with Donald Trump.

They started a conversation and that conversation led to a relationship that ultimately became Donald Trump's newest investor.

The moral of the story: Even Donald Trump needs to be introduced to the right people.

5 Steps To Becoming A Connector

OK, you now buy into becoming a Connector. But how do you get started?

Here are the 5 steps to becoming a Super-Connector with speed and ease:

1. **Get out there.** You will not meet and find good people to introduce to others by being a couch potato with a clicker in your hand. Research high quality locations, events, organizations, and activities. Hang out with quality and you'll be able to connect others with quality.

These are the criteria I look for when connecting people to others:

> ▸ Do they have a generous, willing-to-give attitude? In other
> words, are they generous and thoughtful in their networking?

- Do they offer a product or service of merit and value to the folks in my marketplace? Or to other markets I may interact with?

   For example: If I meet a well-respected professor at a university, he may not have a great deal of importance to my corporate connections. However, to my colleague who coaches high school students on how to get into college, this professor could be a fantastic connection.

- Do they have a good network themselves? Quality people with quality networks have a great deal more appeal in the marketplace.

2. **Ask connections who they would like to meet.** You may think you know, or that it's obvious. Very often people have two categories of people they want to meet: referral sources and end users. As you are building relationships with new colleagues, ask them for details about their ideal referral partners, their sweet spot clients. I often keep a spreadsheet of new colleagues and who their ideal referral partners are and who their ideal clients are.

3. **Connect the dots.** In your networking travels, think "connect the dots."

   Remember the exercise they used in elementary school to teach you relationships of seemingly unrelated objects? There would be an apple and an automobile. Then you would have to identify how these seemingly unrelated items were related.

   It's the same thing when you are "connecting the dots" in business. But to do this most effectively while networking, you will need to "listen like a fox." By listening differently, below the surface, you will soon notice that you are often meeting people whose needs/wants match others' products, services, or interests. Matching the needs and wants of people you meet takes developing that "connect the dots" strategic thinking. Practice will make you effective.

4. **Connect cautiously.** Before you connect two people you think are a good fit, ask both if they'd like to meet one another, and get agreement. Get their permission.

You can either introduce them by email or if you are in close proximity and it adds to the experience, invite both new connections to a meeting or a meal with you. You can facilitate the meeting. When you are present at a connection meeting, your value increases: you've brought two relevant people together, and you've taken the time and made an effort to guide the new relationship into development. These kinds of connection efforts are rarely forgotten.

5. **Extra credit: Follow-up.** In several weeks or months, it's thoughtful to follow-up with the parties you've brought together to see what's emerged from their new relationship. It demonstrates thoughtfulness. And it reinforces the effort you made on their behalf.

CHAPTER 18

How To Network Like
A Fox At Conferences,
Seminars, And Big Events

*You can make more friends in two months by becoming
interested in other people than you can in two years
by trying to get other people interested in you.*
— Dale Carnegie

CAN ANYTHING BE MORE DAUNTING: Getting on an airplane, traveling to a conference, faced with thousands of attendees milling about at exhibition tables, in speaker auditoriums, attending breakout sessions, and seated at tables of strangers for hotel breakfasts, lunches, dinners and cocktail parties?

Whoa!

How can we possibly get a handle on all of this?

Yet, one of the best places to "network like a fox" is at business conferences. But, it depends on which conferences and it depends on how you navigate these conferences.

Which Conferences Should I Go To? And
Which Ones Should I Avoid?

This is a key question people ask me all the time. The answer will best be gained by going back to preparation and research before attending or participating in any networking event.

Remember the 4 Archetypes of Ideal Connections, your Grow Zone?

> Ideal Prospects
> Ideal Introducers and Connectors
> Ideal Referrers
> Ideal "sweet spot" Clients (end users)

When making choices about conferences or events to attend, you will definitely want to determine whether theses 4 Archetypes will be attending as well.

But, suppose you take a different tack than the norm: suppose you plan out first how you might be helpful to these archetypes when you meet them at a conference or an event, then focus on how they can be helpful to you.

While this seems counterintuitive, let's dig a little more deeply into each category and see how you can connect more readily with these ideal folks at conferences, seminars, and anywhere you network.

For each of these connection types, use the ideal client profiler I've provided in the Resources section at the end of the book to help you clearly distinguish who you'd ideally like to meet in each category.

For example, if your ideal prospects are moms returning to the workforce in NYC, use the profiler to help you specify all of this population's characteristics and issues.

This could have a major impact on selecting the conference you attend.

For ideal referrers, what characteristics would these folks have? Would they be general contractors, or lawyers, or teachers, or engineers at big companies, or human resource executives? I once asked a woman who owned a contracting referral service if residential real estate brokers were good referrals for her. That seemed like a pretty logical "connect the dots" assumption. She said, "NO, real estate brokers are not good for me because they like to be hubs of information for their buyer and seller clients. They tend to have their favorites and they connect clients to these folks directly."

Real estate brokers often rely on trust and estates lawyers and on country club/social environments to meet actual buyers and home listers/sellers.

The point here is to really drill down and be specific about the characteristics of each of these categories of people. The clearer you are, the more ideal people you will attract, meet, and grow connected to.

Just the other day, I made a wonderful new connection on LinkedIn. As I do from time to time, just to change things up and test out new strategies, I posted something in my status. A business owner in Indiana contacted me to congratulate me on this status change.

As I usually do, I asked about what was happening in her business and what she was working on. After a couple of back and forth messages, and after I looked at her LinkedIn profile, I gathered that this woman was a corporate trainer in mid-size to large companies focused on leadership, team building, and communications problems. To help me be a better referrer, I asked, "Tell me exactly who your ideal client is, who you want to work with."

Her response: "Any company that has communication problems and needs to repair internal relationships."

This is a typical response by business owners. "Any company" or "Anyone who" is an answer certain to yield zero introductions or referrals.

This response is what I call "the mask of the generalist." You feel shielded and safe by not specifying a niche or an industry because you think you won't miss any opportunities.

In today's market, nothing could be more incorrect.

People need specifics to help them know who you want to meet, who the right referrals are for you. Because everyone is so busy, and sometimes they aren't listening as well as we'd like, if you give them generalities, they will be clueless about exactly whom you would like to meet. When they hear generalities, people usually tune out. Remember, people are not focused on your business; they are focused on their business. Help them help you by making it super easy for them.

Walter is a gentleman I met at a networking referral group meeting. He seemed very nice, professional, and we conscientiously set up a follow-up meeting for the next week.

At our follow-up meeting, I started the conversation by asking Walter a number of probing, open-ended questions about his background, his current business, his services, and his objectives.

It turned out that Walter had a unique background. He had launched a business, lived in Hawaii, and had other distinctive experiences. We got around to discussing his current business, which assists service businesses in retrieving outstanding fees. It is not a standard collections business. Because his business served practices with health insurance billing and payments, I had a client who would be a good referral for him.

I connected them and it was a good relationship. I'm happy to say it ultimately helped my client and did turn out to be a piece of business for Walter.

When Walter attempted to introduce me to people, here's how he connected the dots for me:

He wanted to introduce me to people who do exactly what I do. Not that I mind meeting other consultants. However, I was perplexed. I asked him, "Walter, after I explained whom I work with and who ideal referrers and end-user clients are for me, whom do you think I'd like to meet?"

Walter looked like a deer in the headlights. I could see he had no idea who I really wanted to meet. He was trying to be helpful, but what came to his mind were my competitors because they were similar to me instead of my ideal prospects, referrers, and clients.

Obviously, I wanted to meet my ideal referrers and ideal clients. I also wanted to meet other connectors, but I had hoped Walter had been hearing me.

There are 3 possible explanations for this scenario, which happens time and time again to me and many other professionals.

- ▶ Walter clearly hadn't been listening
- ▶ Walter couldn't connect the dots between what my business is and who my ideal clients are.
- ▶ I didn't specify clearly enough who my ideal connections are.

In this situation I had clearly and specifically told Walter who I would like to be connected with.

My assumption was that he was not listening carefully.

Many people will not understand who you want to meet unless you spell it out for them in a step by step way.

Help them help you by giving them a paint-by-numbers crystal-clear profile of who you're looking for, what you are interested in, and the best situations to be listening for to send people your way.

Clarity Is Key

The level of your clarity about who you want to meet will be directly proportionate to your level of success in choosing the right events to attend, and which ones you should bypass.

Michael is a lawyer. To be specific, he specializes in the area of law called intellectual property, such as trademarks and patents. But Michael has an even more specific specialization: he focuses heavily on helping companies in the medical device space protect their intellectual property.

Michael was a frequent attendee at my professional networking events. One day, we had a catch-up call. I asked him how things were going and how he was doing with his networking. He said, "Pretty well. I get a lot of my business from lawyers in other specializations. But truthfully, I would love to upgrade my networking." My ears perked up. I said, "Really, what do you mean?" He said, "I'd love to be meeting more executives and chief financial officers and general counsel in companies who actually make medical devices."

I immediately went into "connect the dots" mode.

A few computer clicks later, I said, "Michael, I have three organizations who host events that are right up your alley. And, as a matter of fact, a major medical device conference is taking place in California next week."

He said, "Really?"

Michael went into action.

He booked his event registration, bought an airplane ticket, made his hotel reservations and spent 3 days in San Diego meeting his sweet-spot niche market of prospective clients. He met execs from medical device manufacturers, made 6 ideal connections and even met conference organizers who were interested in him speaking at the conference the following year.

Boom!

This was an example of going where your ideal prospects are congregating.

Where Not To Attend

Identifying the conferences to avoid is just as important as identifying the ones to attend, maybe even more so.

Very often logic tells us we should focus on attending conferences in our own field or industry.

Lawyers love to attend lawyer conferences.

Accountants love to attend CPA conferences.

When I first started my business, everyone kept asking me if I was going to attend the International Coaching Federation conference. It didn't seem all that logical to me compared to attending conferences where my ideal clients were going — management and leadership conferences.

Nevertheless, in my second year of business, I caved in and went to Chicago to the biggest conference of coaches.

The conference was huge, and there were hundreds and hundreds of fellow coaches in all specializations, niche markets, and levels of training.

I met some very nice people and attended some interesting breakout sessions.

I spent thousands of dollars on attending this event — between airfare, hotel, conference attendance, meals etc.

I bet you can tell the net-net conclusion of this story. I didn't make one connection that turned into a new strategy or a new client or a new connection to new business or even someone I could collaborate with.

In short, I learned some new ideas for my coaching but I could have read about them or learned about them in a book or even stayed at home and watched videos of the event.

I'm not saying it is meaningless to attend conferences with competitors and fellow professionals.

I am saying that if I weigh the strength of opportunity in attending conferences where my ideal referrers and prospects attend versus attending conferences with my own competitors, it's simply no contest.

> To network like a fox, hang out where your
> ideal niche market is hanging out.

The Roadmap To Conference Success

Wouldn't it be great to know exactly which conferences you should attend, get the best return on your networking investment, and how to leverage your attendance to the max?

To"network like a fox" at conferences and big events, here are 11 key strategies as an attendee. (I will discuss sponsoring and exhibiting separately.)

1. **Determine the right events and conferences.** — Using the 4 archetypes profiler, research where these groups will be attending.

   Ask some of your contacts in each category about the conferences or events they attend and groups they speak to.

   Read trade journals read by your clients and note the conferences advertised, the seminars, and the events listed.

2. **Research the right events.** Using Google to find your ideal conferences and events requires combining keywords.

   For example, suppose you want to be meeting facilities managers of large real estate structures: Conferences + Facilities Managers would bring up events in a variety of locations.

   Or suppose you want to connect with CFO's in large corporations: CFO Management conferences is one search term you could use.

3. **Volunteer at conferences to ramp up visibility** — If you can't swing the high conference registration fees, or you want to accelerate your visibility, donate your time to work on a conference committee.

   Conferences always need extra hands, and by volunteering you may well get the opportunity to attend gratis and meet the leaders by working side by side with them. You can find out a bit about the committees by reading about the organizations or associations previous conference online. They often have a staff or team section where you can learn about the organizations and event leaders.

4. **Preparation makes perfect.** Usually, event organizers will publish the names of the companies attending the event shortly before the event takes place. You want to learn the actual names of attendees within these companies. If the event organizers do not provide this to registrants, contact the sponsorship director or the person listed as the support person online and ask how you can get an attendee list.

   If they do not have one, you can research the companies attending by reading websites. The ideal events to attend are those that do publish an attendee list. Prioritizing the companies/attendees and reading their LinkedIn profiles will give you a terrific starting point for organizing your time at the event. You can connect with people on LinkedIn and invite them for coffee while at the event. Remember to avoid being pitchy or salesy beforehand. Keep it friendly, light. You can suggest meeting at one of the cocktail parties or breakout sessions.

5. **Create a Roadmap for the event.** Organize your time for attending keynote speeches, breakout sessions, private one-on-one meetings with targeted attendees, meal times and social cocktail parties. Mix it up, but keep your eye on Networking Up and meeting the decision makers. (The Network Like A Fox Action Guide contains specific tools and implementation exercises.)

6. **Meet decision makers** even if you're not a big cheese. A key goal is to Network Up and meet the top level event organizers. You want them to be aware of you for future speaking and leadership opportunities.

   Your ideal client decision makers may often be found sponsoring, speaking, hosting happy hours, and leading breakout sessions. This one tip often stumps people. They know who they want to meet but don't know what to say to open a dialogue with decision makers. Launching into your pitch is the fastest way to squelch opportunity.

   When meeting decision makers or speakers at an event, share one thing you liked about the decision maker's speech, or because you've researched their company website, tell this decision maker one thing that interested you about what their company is doing. I like using the "kill two birds with one stone" technique: tell the decision maker you are writing a blog post about their area of expertise and ask if you might interview them. That's often a very powerful magnet. It gives the decision maker something vs. asks something of them, and almost always, decision makers feel flattered by a request to be interviewed on topics in their areas of expertise. It also gives you permission to set up a follow-up appointment with him or her.

One of my favorite stories is about a very talented lady who smartly connected with and won over her ideal decision makers at a major trade show. Meet Nirmala Narine.

CASE STUDY
Nirmala Narine
Founder of Global Living and
Dish Network Spice Celebrity

Spicing Up Her World
By Meeting The Right People

Nirmala Narine's world for the first several years of her life was a tiny kitchen in Guyana with no running water or electricity. Even as a child, Nirmala was drawn to food and flavors. Today, she is founder and "spice master" of Nirmala's Kitchen, a gourmet importer and distributor of exotic ingredients.

If you visit Nirmala's website, www.nirmalaskitchen.com, you almost expect to smell the wonderful aromas of the many spices and recipes she concocts out of the ingredients harvested from the earth. But don't be fooled by the domestic bent to her creations. Nirmala is one very sharp business person.

Visit her press page and you will see she travels in some of the most well-respected culinary circles.

When she first began her quest to build a business around spices, Nirmala wondered how she was going to be discovered by the right food experts.

Then she realized, go where the food experts go: The Fancy Food Show in NYC.

There, she networked with many food experts. After the show, she thoughtfully sent some scrumptious samples to The New York Times Food Editor. This led to a personal meeting with the editor, who loved Nirmala's flavors so much, she introduced her to her good friend Eric Ripert,

Executive Chef/ Co-owner of Le Bernardin. Eric sampled her innovative spice blends and immediately invited her to add her food flair to his team. Now, Nirmala's influence is tasted by some of the most discerning clients at Le Bernadin. Martha Stewart has sung her praises as well.

Nirmala understood how important it was to pique the taste interests of the decision-makers in the food world. She sent samples to the right people, researched and reached out to book publishers who had successfully produced best-selling cookbooks and endeared herself to them through her powerful products and positive spirit.

At the celebration party of her first cookbook, a friend of a friend brought a friend. Nirmala met Michael Chapman, a well-connected man with a network including presidents and leaders of major corporations. Michael introduced Nirmala to a friend who was a research executive at Pepsi.

Now, as luck would have it, Nirmala was crazy about Pepsi. As a child in Guyana, Pepsi was a rare treat for children. When she met the Pespi executive, they got to talking about Nirmala's childhood passion for Pepsi. One conversation led to another.... Ultimately, Nirmala was invited by Pepsi to work on developing new flavors.

Nirmala's clients now include many of the most well-known and influential in the culinary field and she has attracted leaders of major organizations who want to tap her innovative ideas on flavor and cuisine.

When you talk to Nirmala, you learn not only about her love for flavors and spices, but her passion for people. Especially the right people.

7. **Build Quick Rapport with decision makers** — See item 4. Make sure you are knowledgeable about the decision maker before you meet him/her (research). Today you can do this on the fly — pull up their LinkedIn profile while they are speaking — it's that fast! When to meet them is also an important decision. Right after they are speaking is often not good because they are being hounded by a lot of people who rush up after they finish. Maybe say hello and shake their hand as they are leaving the room.

    And remember Keith Ferrazzi's story? OK, maybe you don't want to (or would be arrested) by following someone into the men's room to build rapport. But by being resourceful you can walk over to decision makers with grace. Confidence will make a huge difference when meeting decision makers.

    Remember, everyone is nervous meeting new people. (I'll be providing Connecting With Big Cheese scripts in the Network Like A Fox Action Guide)

8. **Listen for Unexpected Opportunities.** As strategic as business can be, there are the wonderful moments of real unexpected opportunity that make it so much fun and exciting. You might be talking to a random attendee completely off your event roadmap. And then you hear of something that's happening in this person's firm or company that completely aligns with something you're working on. Or an offhand complaint comes out that is right up your alley. LISTEN. But listen from a completely different context; listen between the words and lines. If you train your brain to connect dots, new opportunities emerge.

9. **Follow-Up Like A Fox.** Review Follow-Up Like A Fox strategies and implement them fast. People get very busy after several days away at a conference. I usually adhere to the First 30-Minutes Rule — follow-up with new contacts within a 1/2 hour of an event. In the case of conferences, I recommend following up within 1 week, but the sooner the better. The idea is to follow-up with a next step or some reason to stay in touch. Suggest a phone call or a meeting if geography allows. My tip sheet, The Fortune Is In The Follow-Up Tip Sheet (www.thebusinessfox.com) will give you 33 ideas you can use to follow-up with new contacts.

10. **Leverage the event into future speaking engagements.** This is an important strategy. Imagine meeting 30 or 40 of your ideal prospective clients all at once — with you being at the front of the room leading a panel discussion or a presentation! That's the power of delivering speaking engagements to your ideal niche market. The leaders of program management are often at the conference. You can even ask at the information booth if the program director is at the event and who he or she is. It's a very smart idea to seek this person out and introduce yourself to him or her. Do something nice for them and they will remember you for next year's conference or for local or regional events. Sometimes you can begin speaking at regional events and move up to national ones.

When Should You Exhibit Or Sponsor At A Conference?

Being an exhibitor or a sponsor can be an extremely effective lead generation tactic if done at the right events and in the right ways.

Clients of mine, whose niche market is the home heating oil industry, had been exhibiting at home heating oil conferences every year. Consistently, they talked to a lot of people, but they weren't really tracking what their conference ROI was.

They didn't have a measurement or tracking strategy.

They didn't have a follow-up strategy.

They spent all their time planning for the fantastic table they would set up, and how they would talk to the attendees that visited the table.

They spent virtually no time planning how to turn connections into leads or how they would follow-up after the event.

As we worked together, they created a roadmap: the strategy leading up to the event, researched attendees and other sponsors, created a set of goals for capturing email addresses of visitors to their exhibit so they could start to communicate with contacts and leads via email and e-newsletters, and crafted a full-blown follow-up strategy.

This resulted in a successful email marketing campaign that not only brought new business but demonstrated to their prospective clients how online marketing should be done.

Too many business people get enthused by the notion of visibility at an event. They don't map out how to fully leverage it.

When Should You Sponsor?

You should consider sponsoring when you have the financial resources to invest in big-picture visibility.

Sponsoring is usually more of a PR endeavor vs. a lead generation effort. Sponsoring allows you to receive recognition repeatedly because often your company name will be on the event program, you will receive signage throughout the banners at the event, and sometimes it will afford you saying a few words at different sub-events throughout the conference.

Sponsoring is a broader approach to marketing. That being said, "sponsoring like a fox" could bring fantastic leads your way if you follow-up properly with people.

When Should You Buy An Exhibit Table
At A Trade Show Or Conference?

An exhibit table is a sales effort. It puts you among other "vendors" and is directed at lead generation. It is designed for you to have a gentle sales conversation with those who are visiting your table or booth. It is an excellent way for you to leverage the one-to-many approach — becoming visible to lots of category-specific or niche-specific people in a short window of time.

The key here is driving traffic to your booth. Some trade shows or conferences will allow you to buy advertising about your booth so you can alert potential buyers or visitors and entice them to look for your table at the event.

Then you will also have to be innovative and creative about spreading the word and enticing people to come to visit your booth. Just because you have a booth does not ensure you will have visitors. You have to be a visitor-magnet through smart marketing.

One of the savviest networkers around is my colleague and friend Marcia Nelson, Practice Growth Manager at Anchin, Block & Anchin LLP. Not only is she a fantastic Connector, she wins the prize for being clever and attracting lots of people to stop at her exhibit table at big events. Then she chats them up and starts building rapport. She shares her exhibit success secrets here:

CASE STUDY
Marcia Nelson
Networker Extraordinaire,
Practice Growth Manager
Anchin, Block & Anchin LLP

Exhibiting Trade Secrets for
Meeting The Right People At Trade Shows

As a manager of business growth for a major professional services firm, I spend a fair amount of my time sitting behind a booth at trade shows collecting business cards, which I can then add to my database and, hopefully, eventually, turn those cards into business down the road.

But first things first — with some fierce competition out there, my main goal is to get people to stop at my booth, and then I can take it from there.

#1 Get A Gimmick. In the words of Gypsy Rose Lee, "you gotta have a gimmick." Hats, pens, beanie babies, notepads, an overflowing candy dish or a popcorn machine — whatever it is that you choose, it must be something that stands out from the crowd. Why? Chances are that the competitor in the booth next to you has the same thing, or worse, something better. I have a favorite cookie vendor that I use because the cookies are bite size, come in unusual flavors, and are so delicious that when someone walks by and randomly grabs one, he inevitably turns around and comes back for seconds, and then I've got his attention and can talk about what I really sell.

#2 Location, location, location. Not every tradeshow lets you choose your location in advance, but it never hurts to ask to see a floor plan and pick a good spot. Prime locations include near the front door, next to the coffee station, or on the end of a long row. It helps if you sign up early, so plan ahead, and give the sponsor a list of your competitors and ask that you NOT be placed next to them. One final hint — if you know who some of the other vendors are, ask to be placed near another firm (not a competitor) that you know will generate a lot of traffic. You may be able to capture some of the overflow.

#3 Have a drawing. At the last show I attended there were drawings for massages, restaurants, ipods, and remote control cars. I like to hold a drawing for gift certificates — they're easy to mail to the recipient at the end of the show, and they appeal across the board. The amount has to be significant enough to get someone to drop their business card — hey, they know you're going to add them to your mailing list, so there must be an incentive — so $50 is a good starting amount for most shows, but I've done them for amounts up to $500 if it's a big show with a lot of competition.

#4 Just keep smiling. No one is going to stop by your booth if you're spending all your time with your eyes glued to your Smartphone, or if you scowl at anyone who walks by. By the end of a week-long trade show, the muscles in my face hurt from smiling, but I've gotten business from the last person to walk by my booth and talk to me.

Once you've gathered all those business cards, then the real follow-up fun can begin!

By the way, Marcia's teenage daughter says Marcia's job is to "take people to lunch."

Exhibitors' tables are usually less costly than sponsorships, although this will depend on the different sponsorship packages and levels offered by the event organizers. Sometimes, event organizers will permit two businesses to share a booth. This can make good budget sense if the two companies are complementary — serving the same market but not competitive in terms of services or products.

The Why Of Exhibiting

- ▶ You want to exhibit when you know you are speaking directly to your ideal niche market decision makers.
- ▶ You want to exhibit when you want to generate many leads in a short period of time.
- ▶ You want to exhibit when you can afford the time to be there at the event or hire or send really strong people to man the booth.
- ▶ You want to exhibit if you are prepared for a solid follow-up effort; it can take several days to follow-up after the event.
- ▶ You want to exhibit if you are willing to invest the time and dollars, and track how many real leads, relationships, and new business ultimately come out of this.
- ▶ You want to exhibit when you are ready and capable of devoting booth design and planning for how your booth will look, have signage made, and creating a clear strategy for how you will attract people to the booth, and then how you will engage them and build rapport and interest in your services or products.

A Few Final Conference Words Of Wisdom

1. **Don't hang out with people you know at conferences.** Concentrate on meeting new people. Optimize your time.

2. **Attend as many VIP events as your budget and time will allow.** This is where the influencers and decision makers are hanging out.

Get there early. The VIP's usually have to arrive at the event early, so if you get there early and they get there early, you can easily connect with them before the masses arrive. Easy to Network Up.

3. **Volunteer at the conference to save the conference fee.** If the registration fee is out of your budget, or you are not ready to exhibit, volunteer to work on the conference. Conference organizers never have enough hands to manage conference details. Offer to help or contribute something. They may invite you to attend gratis if you volunteer or contribute something they need and want.

4. **Go on VIP conference tours.** Some well-organized conferences have what are called VIP Conference Tours to show you how to get the most out of the conference.

5. **Help spread the word about the conference.** Use your social media activities and posts to help the conference organizers promote and spread the word about the event. Every conference organizer appreciates people who help them promote the event and increase attendance.

Parting Thoughts

I HOPE THAT BY reading this book your view about networking has been at least a little transformed.

The information and tips were designed to give you a new way to approach building your network with strategy and thoughtfulness.

The case study stories were intended to inspire you and give you some real-world examples of how, when we network in targeted ways, with strategy and intention, great things can happen.

One of the most important networking lessons I have learned over the years is how our connections are forever.

The shelf life of a connection is forever — or at least as long as you both are alive.

There is never too much time between phone calls or get togethers for amazing possibility to open up between people.

My friend and colleague, Bonnie Low Kramen (whom I met through networking, of course) has adopted this philosophy and it has changed her life in unimaginable ways.

CASE STUDY
Bonnie Low-Kramen
Former Personal Assistant To Olympia Dukakis

How "Who You Know" Opened The Right Door
To The Rest Of My Life

Mine is a classic case of how "who you know" opened the right door that changed my life forever.

In the early 80's, I had worked as Box Office Manager at the Alley Theatre in Houston, TX. One of my close colleagues was the telemarketing manager, Jeffrey Orth. Then, I moved back to my home state of NJ. I hadn't seen Jeffrey in a long while so when he came up to New York City on a vacation, I made certain that we carved out some time together. We met for a drink on 42nd St. He brought his good friend with him, Scott Michaels, who at the time was the Marketing Director for the Whole Theatre in Montclair, NJ. Over this drink, Scott told me that they needed a PR Director at the theatre and asked me if I would like to apply.

The easy thing would have been to say no because I had never done publicity before. But because my degree was in English and I had already spent 5 years working in theatres, I made a "big leap" decision that I could do the job.

No one was hired at the theatre without first being interviewed by the Producing Artistic Director. I went to my interview with the PAD, and met her as she was sitting on top of the copy machine wearing ripped jeans. I remember her firm handshake and strong, beautiful face. It took about one minute for me to understand how very smart this woman was. I was going to have to be on my "A" game all the time. We hit it off and I was hired on the spot — by Olympia Dukakis.

In January, 1986, Olympia was not yet famous, so we began our working relationship under "normal people" circumstances. Within 10 months, however, Olympia announced that she was going to Canada for a month — to shoot the movie MOONSTRUCK. One Oscar later, the rest is history and the phone hasn't stopped ringing. I became Olympia's personal executive assistant and we worked together for 25 years until August 11, 2011.

Meeting Scott and making this "big leap" decision altered my world as I knew it.

This experience showed me without a doubt how important it is to meet and interact with the "right people." It's why I make it a point to continue to attend functions and introduce myself. I have met people who have helped me not only with my work with Olympia, but with New York Celebrity Assistants Association, in which I am a leader, and even helping colleagues find work. When someone learns I worked with Olympia Dukakis, calls get returned and other doors open. At the same time, it is important to not abuse the power.

I've learned that keeping relationships going is so important. Opportunities might not be there today, but what about the next day or next year? That's what happened with my friend Jeffrey who years later introduced me to Scott who introduced me to Olympia.

One thing that I think is challenging for people is to have confidence with influential people when they are just starting out. One way to overcome this challenge is to recognize that, with the working world filled with mediocrity, standing out and performing with excellence and generosity will get you noticed by influencers.

Also, people love to talk. Your reputation goes around in a flash so only give them reasons to say positive things.

People often ask me how they can become more influential and appeal to other influencers. I see two qualities as essential: Confidence and clarity in communication. I also believe in mentorship. Actively seek to have one or more and seek to BE a mentor to others. Everyone has something of value to teach.

I understand that it can be intimidating to be with very rich, successful, smart people. But…what I found was that I could talk about the things that I knew a great deal about and they were interested! Also, be curious! People LOVE talking about themselves so ask questions and LEARN!

I always sought to improve myself. I read a great deal to improve my vocabulary and depth of knowledge. Education is critical. Upgrade your wardrobe and hairstyle at least once a year. Take a hard look at what you bring to the table with your skill set and outward appearance. The most successful people I know look and sound the part.

Today, I am using my experience in connecting with high-quality influencers as I launch my educational "Be the Ultimate Assistant" curriculum for professional assistants. Now, my passion is about the success of professional working women in a very tough economy and I am strategically connecting with leaders in the recruitment arena to help further my mission. I believe in paying it forward.

This paraphrased quote from JFK sums up the best advice I can give professionals and business people regarding connecting successfully:

"Ask not what they can do for you but
what you can do for them."

So what I hope you take out of this book are some smarter, more intentional ways to meet the right people, some smarter ways for you to help the right people, and ways you can build relationships that reward you for years to come.

Some time back, I read this quote by Tim Sanders, and it just stuck with me.

"Your network is your net worth."

It is my hope that this book vastly increases your net worth in all ways.

Stay strategic, stay connected.

(Thanks for letting me riff off of Steve Jobs)

Nancy Fox's Reading List

WHEN I FIRST STARTED building my business and networking, I read every networking book I could get my hands on.

I learned a great deal, but some became my mega-highlighted favorites.

These books changed my world forever.

How To Win Friends And Influence People
Dale Carnegie

The 7 Habits of Highly Effective People
Stephen Covey

Dig Your Well Before You're Thirsty
Harvey Mackay

Never Eat Alone
Keith Ferrazzi

Networking With The Affluent
Thomas Stanley

The Introvert Advantage
Marti Olsen Laney

Smart Networking
Liz Lynch

The Tipping Point
Malcolm Gladwell

Think And Grow Rich
Napoleon Hill

Network Like A Fox
Grow Zone Profiler

Ideal Client	Ideal Client Characteristics
Industries, verticals, types of businesses	
Geographic preferences	
Sweet spot business size (revenue, number of employees, etc.)	
Client role/Decision Maker: President, CEO, VP Sales, Business Owner, etc	
Gender	
Socio-economic sector	
Education	
Personality style: extrovert, introvert, high energy, etc.	
Values	
Business Style	
What kind of service providers are they looking for?	
Decision making style	
Where are they networking, speaking, attending conferences?	
Other	

Ideal Prospective Client	Ideal Prospect Characteristics
Industries, verticals, types of businesses	
Geographic preferences	
Sweet spot business size (revenue, number of employees, etc.)	
Client role/Decision Maker: President, CEO, VP Sales, Business Owner, etc	
Gender	
Socio-economic sector	
Education	
Personality style: extrovert, introvert, high energy, etc.	
Values	
Business Style	
What kind of service providers are they looking for?	
Decision making style	
Where are they networking, speaking, attending conferences?	
Other	

Ideal Referrer	Ideal Referrer Characteristics
Industries, verticals, types of businesses	
Geographic preferences	
Sweet spot business size (revenue, number of employees, etc.)	
Client role/Decision Maker: President, CEO, VP Sales, Business Owner, etc	
Gender	
Socio-economic sector	
Education	
Personality style: extrovert, introvert, high energy, etc.	
Values	
Business Style	
What kind of service providers are they looking for?	
Decision making style	
Where are they networking, speaking, attending conferences?	
Other	

Ideal Introducer/Connector	Ideal Introducer Characteristics
Industries, verticals, types of businesses	
Geographic preferences	
Sweet spot business size (revenue, number of employees, etc.)	
Client role/Decision Maker: President, CEO, VP Sales, Business Owner, etc	
Gender	
Socio-economic sector	
Education	
Personality style: extrovert, introvert, high energy, etc.	
Values	
Business Style	
What kind of service providers are they looking for?	
Decision making style	
Where are they networking, speaking, attending conferences?	
Other	

Other Business Fox Books & Courses

Network Like A Fox Action Guide

Make Rain Without The Pain

Turn Your Rich Niche Into A Business Cash Machine

Speak And Grow Your Business

T.O.P.P. Networking Training System

Available at www.thebusinessfox.com/learningchannel

About Nancy Fox

NANCY FOX has been a business coach and consultant since 1999. Following a successful corporate career as a senior marketing executive, she has coached hundreds of business owners and professionals in business development, networking, niche marketing, and sales, guiding them to breakthrough levels of success.

As a networking passionista and specialist, she co-launched a highly successful professional networking event, Metro Roundtable NYC, bringing hundreds of top tier service professionals together and guiding them in cross-marketing and referring high-level new business.

Bitten by the social networking bug early on, and experiencing smashing business growth through online networking and marketing, Nancy blended her enthusiasm for all things digital with business strategy and networking and launched The Business Fox Network for entrepreneurs and professionals.

Nancy has been featured and quoted in *Business Week, The New York Times, The Daily News, CBS Money Watch,* and has spoken at Rotary Clubs, national franchising conferences, and has led masterminds and workshops nationwide.

She now lives in Los Angeles with her dog Baxter but loves to travel to Paris, Italy, and video-skype with colleagues, clients, and friends all over the world.